Humble Heroes

Visit www.booksurge.com to order additional copies.

STEVEN GEORGE BUSTIN

HUMBLE HEROES

HOW THE USS NASHVILLE CL43 FOUGHT WWII

2007

Humble Heroes

CONTENTS

***

USS Nashville in mid-war camouflage, official US Navy Photo

IN APPRECIATION

This book has truly been a four year labor born of love, respect, and admiration. It has been an endeavor of 98% research and 2% writing. And it has been a widely collaborative effort in the sense that it would never have been written without the encouragement, support, assistance, graciousness, and extreme generosity of many wonderful people.

I want to thank my family for their constant support and encouragement. My niece Katy Mae Nickle helped convince me the book would be of interest to more than simply my immediate family and provided helpful transcription services. My mother, Kathleen Bustin, showed unwavering faith in my ability to see it through to completion in time for the 2006 reunion in Washington, D.C. and taught me as a child that anything was possible if you wanted it. Gigi and I were married during this project and she provided unending support and understanding in my often times selfish determination to isolate myself in order to research and write. My sister Annie Bustin always reminded me at the right times that our father, who passed away prior to the beginning of this project, would be proud and was watching my progress. My cousin Michael Nickle provided the support of someone who knew how painful writing a story of this nature can be. My nephew Daniel Nickle motivated me with his amazement and enthusiasm that his grandfather was part of such a big story. My Uncle, Charles Hellams reminded me that such men were special and needed their story told. My brother-in-law William Bush showed great appreciation for the crew and my efforts. My mother-in-law Joan Bailin's frequent inquiries were always a source of motivation.

I cannot possibly mention each and every person of the hundreds that provided great assistance, somewhat out of fear I may leave someone off the list, especially among the scores of crew members and their families who are the true authors of this book. But there are those who went "above and beyond" in making the book viable. My first in person contact with any source of information was with the long time gatekeepers of the reunion, Ed "Bulldog" Remler and his wife Audrey. The often visited Remler home in Overland Park, Kansas includes a built out basement that is in essence, a USS Nashville library, bulging with photos, flags, letters, rosters, clippings, books, and the like. For many years the Remlers would load up the entire collection and bring it to the reunions. I stayed with the Remlers for several days, enjoying their genuine hospitality, and was able to truly jumpstart the book with their on-hand archives.

The current and past few reunions have been expertly handled by Don and Goldie Hill. They have been instrumental in providing me access to so many articles of information, introducing me to the entire reunion association, shepherding me through many processes and inquiries from outside the organization, warmly welcoming me to the Nashville family, and bestowing upon me the greatest of compliments by considering me an "honorary member of the Nashville crew." Their assistance and support was indispensable.

The entire reunion association membership was invaluable, each person I talked to or received emails or letters from, solicited and not. Of notable assistance have been Patrick Carigan, Billie Ray Lyerly, Albert U. Gaines, Leonard Meyer, Joe Mills, Robert Shafer, Richard Metcalf, W. Frank Gill, Ron Neff, Edward Fitzgerald, Fred Grider, Marie Clifton, Agnes Kahut, James Clark, John Bosier, Edna Pearl Champion, William Banks, Jr., Ralph Piper, Helen Naumowicz, Maury Jack Wood, Paul Taloff, Richard Smith, Samuel Sanders, Peggy Reilly, Richard Egles, Stephen Saradin, Henry Van Wagner, J. D Baccus, Joseph Fales, Vivian Garbak, Joseph Graves, Emil Machrone, Allan Ensor, John Cotton, Harold Landry, Norval Marion Jacks, Jr., Leon Higginson, Donn Ashley, Charles Conrad, Walter Benson, Raymond D. Chaney, Harry J. Grocki, John H. Carmichael, Harry Nadeau, Edward Yusko, Charles Reilly, Frances Patrick, William Holmes, Gerald T. Jones, Arden Sanderson, Harold G. O'Hara, Albert L. Pender, William Smith, Rufus B. Thompson, Clarence Smith, Joseph Marion, Elvin Crockett, Wilbur Bunker, Lawrence Cavanaugh, Clarence Czarnecki, Lawrence G. Spencer, Paul McCarty, Roberta McKinnell, Ron Nickerson, Morris Short, Clayton Snow, Warren Longhurst, Joe Juarez, Richard Jordan, George Huffstetler, Jack Hubbard, Allen Ensor, Robert Easley, John Dykstra, Henry Bittner, Walter Benson, Nancy Ashley, Charles Conrad, W. Frank Gill, Albert

A. Murray, Charles Norman, Richard Marelli, Frances Patrick, Lester L. Morton, Jr., Richard P. Walsh, Albert Landi, Ronald M. Neff, Alex Zdurne, Delbert Ford, John Carmichael, Michael Reese, Patrick Purdue, Hugh Patrick, Alfonso Garcia Vejar, Ed Roiek, Clarence D. Bivins, J.R. Clifton, Arvel F. Gearing, Bob Zuck, Bev Bevington, George Massetti, John Hane, and many, many more.

Many people were generous with photographs but particularly so was Joe Mills who took so many of the ones in this book himself.

Michael Reese and his creative team from Atlas Media Group of Ames, IA contributed first class cover design and photo restoration services.

I also wish to thank the late author, Tomoe Ishikawa Doss for her professional translations of Japanese to English.

This Book Is Dedicated To My Father, George Leland Joseph Bustin, Gunner's Mate 2nd Class United States Navy 1941-1947, My Mother Kathleen Bustin, A Real Life Rosie The Riveter At The Age Of Fifteen, The Crew Of The USS Nashville, And All Those Who Served In Uniform And On The Home Front During WWII. Their Sacrifice And Gift Of Freedom To Future Generations Is Immeasurable.

PREFACE

***

T he Pacific Theater in WWII was America's second priority, after the European Theater of operations. Despite the fact that America was brought into the war by the shameful Japanese attack on the US naval base at Pearl Harbor and that the Japanese captured ten times the amount of territory the Germans did, Roosevelt and the War Department rightly felt that America's first priority must be saving Britain and defeating Nazi Germany and Fascist Italy, while maintaining the fight in the Pacific against the Japanese until the industrial might of the country could adequately supply both. Hence, the war in the Pacific saw America operate in the role of underdog in men, material, and experience until well past the Battle of Midway.

By the end of the war the Pacific was akin to an American lake. More than 90% of the naval vessels afloat on the planet were American, as America's shipyards turned out carriers, battleships, cruisers, destroyers, submarines, and a multitude of support and landing craft during the war. But during the early dark months, devoid of victory, with much of the American fleet resting in the mud of Pearl Harbor, ships and men of the line were in dangerously short supply. Few of those early brave vessels survived service throughout the war. The Nashville was one of them, serving from the first day to the last, and beyond.

The USS Nashville, CL-43, a Brooklyn Class light cruiser, was awarded ten Battle Stars during WWII, more than any other Brooklyn Class cruiser. She and her crew served from the North Atlantic to the South Pacific, from the Aleutians to China, and almost everyplace in between. Her keel laid down on January 24, 1935 and commissioned on June 6, 1938, the ship and her crew served with great heroism and effectiveness throughout the entire war. Like other light cruisers, she was designed to defend smaller vessels, be a sole raiding force due to her power and speed, scout dangerously ahead of main task forces, provide support bombardment, and serve as a ship of the line during enemy naval engagements. She did all of this and far more than her designers had envisioned. There are no cruisers turned museum in the United States, unlike carriers, battleships, Liberty ships, a range of others, and even a Higgins boat. Of the forty-seven American light cruisers that battled the enemy in WWII, each and every one that survived the war was sold or unceremoniously cut into scrap.

She is not the best known of the multitude of famous US Navy ships of WWII marketed into public consciousness, great ships like Enterprise, Hornet, Arizona, and Missouri, all of which are museums or a national cemetery in the case of the ill-fated Arizona. In fact, Nashville is not famous or known at all unless you are a student of history in general, and most likely only of US Navy history of WWII. Yet, she served her country and crew well, fought against heavy odds, secretly transported $25 million in British gold bullion, participated in one of the most daring raids in US Navy history sinking the first Japanese surface vessels of the war as a result of offensive action, acted as flagship for General McArthur in his return to the Philippines, survived a devastating direct hit by a kamikaze, and eventually brought US troops home from the war. Her crew took heavy casualties but most returned home safely to start families and go about their lives without most people knowing their wartime experiences. These men, like others of the so-called Greatest Generation, waited half a century in many cases before they learned to share, ever so humbly, their wartime experiences not only with a younger generation, but in many cases with their own families. And what they have collectively shared is certainly but a fragment of their experiences. Hence, the story of the Nashville is typical of US Navy ships serving in the Pacific Theater during WWII.

This book is the story of her crew, a community of more than 1,000 men in harm's way, which in turn is the story of, in one way or another, all US servicemen and women of WWII, a story of the everyday heroism of getting the job done when America needed them. As Nashville crewman Marine Corporal Don Hill put it, "We had a job to do and we did it, and we put in a lot of overtime doing it." It was a ship that bound young men together in ways few, if any, had foreseen at the time. Fully sixty years after the end of the war, the few crewmen alive and able to do so traveled to their latest reunion. Their feelings were perhaps best summed up by one old salt who said, "I never felt love in my life like I did from the crew of the Nashville."

I had the privilege and pleasure of meeting many of the surviving Nashville crew during the writing of this book, and of talking on the phone or exchanging letters and emails with even more. Their passion for life, tenacity in meeting challenges, humor in dealing with physical and emotional pain, and camaraderie among themselves were easily evident. But their most telling, encompassing, and impressive characteristic was their sincere humbleness about their service during the war. All of these men, most who were teenagers at the time, played an integral role in the winning of the war. All of them were in danger at various times and all of them saw the grotesqueness of death during war. Many displayed stunning acts of heroism in defense of their ship and the care of their shipmates. Yet never once during hundreds of conversations did I hear a boastful remark from a crew member in regards to his role and actions. They were proud and boastful about the ship and their crewmates, never about themselves. They truly were, and are, humble heroes.

CHAPTER 1
Buildup: Shakedown

***

"You know, although this was a new ship, it seemed we were constantly painting some part of it."
-Rich Egles

***

The USS Nashville was a ship of the so-called "Treaty Navy," meaning it was authorized, built, and commissioned after the Washington Naval Conference of 1921-22 and the subsequent London Naval Conferences of 1935-36 and prior to 1938. Treaty ships were part of an honest but ultimately naïve attempt to restrict global naval arms races and to legislate enough restrictive parity as to prevent war. It was the Treaty Navy that stood forth alone against the Axis onslaught prior to 1942 when the first ripples of a great wave of American production sent endless numbers and types of ships to fight. Technically, while Nashville was designed under the restrictions of the aforementioned treaty, the ship was in fact a child of President Franklin Roosevelt's New Deal program, specifically the National Recovery Act. In a sense, Nashville was a public works program (as were sister light cruisers Brooklyn, Savannah, and Philadelphia) and fittingly so as a ship of men born of the Great Depression. These new types of cruisers were designed to carry out extended combat operations across vast distances due to the dearth of American bases, relative to the Japanese and British, across the Pacific. This was truly design with future vision and was later put to good use by Nashville and like ships.

The Washington Naval Treaty increased America's interest in light cruisers with great firepower. This new Brooklyn Class had fifteen of the greatly improved six-inch guns with heavy shells and was capable of an astounding rate of fire for the period. It had the greatest firepower of any of the treaty cruisers of any country.

In regard to comparable cruisers of the Japanese, the Brooklyn Class cruisers were far superior in terms of durability, ruggedness, and reliability, and in the case of ruggedness, surprisingly so considering their relatively light armor, armor that Nashville would test during the coming war.

The USS Nashville CL43 (Cruiser Light) was built by New York Shipbuilding Corporation in Camden, New Jersey. Her keel was laid down January 24, 1935. Sponsored by Misses Ann and Mildred Stahlman of Nashville, Tennessee, she was launched October 2, 1937, something akin to the birth of a ship among old salts, and commissioned June 6, 1938 under the command of Captain William W. Wilson. A commissioning of a ship formally transfers the responsibility of the ship to the captain and crew. A formal ceremony is held on the quarterdeck with due pomp and circumstance, orders assigning the ship to the fleet are read, the "Star Spangled Banner" is played, the ensign hoisted, and the captain assumes command as the very first duties, including watch, are initiated. In effect, the ship joins the Navy as a fighting vessel with all of the responsibilities inherent in a Navy ship regardless of time in service to the country.

Nashville, as originally built, was 608 feet, four inches in length, had a beam of sixty-one feet, eight inches, displaced 9,475 tons with a mean draft of nineteen feet, two inches, and could travel at 32.5 knots. The original crew complement was 816 men and fifty-two officers. As built, she stood with fifteen six-inch guns, eight five-inch guns, and eight fifty caliber anti-aircraft guns. Anti-aircraft (AA) guns added during the war, along with technology added 2,000 tons to the weight of the Nashville and other Brooklyn Class cruisers. She was originally widely recognized as a beautiful ship, sleek and trim, not yet burdened with the extra AA and camouflage that the war would add, painted battleship gray but with highly polished brass fittings known as "brightwork," brilliant white lifelines and a stunning teak deck that men like Joe Fales holystoned weekly. There was a hint of luxury and glamour about the ship.

As tradition dictates, the original crew of a ship is forever known as "Plankies" and so it was with the Nashville crew. One of those Plankies was John. H. Carmichael. "We had office space furnished by the New York Shipbuilding Company to prepare the ship's organization, assigning billets to the crew. Officers got housing from the local economy, enlisted men were housed at the Navy Shipyard across the Delaware River." Some men, like Plankie Rich Egles, received their boot camp training right there at the Brooklyn Navy Yard. Egles remembers, "The first thing I had to get used to was sleeping in a hammock. We didn't sleep in a bed or a bunk while we were in training. The hammock would hang about three feet off the floor between two posts. The tighter the hammock was strung up the straighter your body could lie in it. I had a buddy who fell out of his hammock just about every night. During the day it was rolled up and lashed tightly between the posts. It looked like a big hotdog but it had to be done neatly and properly." Plankie Edward Fitzgerald remembers the Nashville as "new, clean, and beautiful." And Albert C. Garbak, who advanced through the ranks from Seaman 2c to Storekeeper 2c to Chief Storekeeper to Acting Pay Clerk to Warrant Officer, was also a proud Plankie. The crew was about to start an intense and prolonged lifelong bonding process that only youthful enthusiasm, danger, and teamwork can produce.

Nashville sailed on calm seas for a short trip to Philadelphia for fitting out then departed Philadelphia on July 19, 1938 to load ammunition and stores in Norfolk, Virginia, never far from land and in deep ocean water. On July 29 she officially started her shakedown cruise and training with Caribbean trips to Guantanamo, Cuba, and Gonaives, Haiti. Plankie W. Frank Gill was on board as Seaman 2c at the time and remembers the gunnery practice at Guantanamo. "We fired thirty-caliber machine guns at a target that was placed against a dusty bank. The wind blew the dust right back into our faces." Plankie Rich Egles was "impressed by the very mountainous beauty I was seeing. Being from New Jersey, I also found extremely hot temperatures, but we were able to get some time to swim and cool off. You know, although this was a new ship, it seemed we were constantly painting some part of it. I think the Navy is famous for its painters and scrubbers." And so it is. Egles and others would soon realize firsthand why Popeye had such large forearms.

Continuing training, Nashville sailed on her first goodwill and deep ocean crossing trip with a visit to Cherbourg, France on August 24, surely the first foreign country most of the crew had ever visited if they did not get liberty in Cuba and Haiti. While docked at the Cherbourg pier the locals would come out at night, some in their finest dress, and stand patiently and longingly and watch the movies that were projected against a jerry-rigged large canvas on the fantail. Both locals and crew would shout questions about the other across the dock, some in English, some in French, and some in a bastardized version and combination of both. The French were mostly interested in Hollywood and cowboys, the crew, in girls, directions (specifically to wherever the girls might be), and some museums too, of course. But shouts across moorings and piers were no substitute for experiencing the local life in person. Many men received liberty and took full advantage of the opportunity. Teenagers from small Kansas farms, hardscrabble Chicago tenements, sweltering Baltimore rowhouses, and dusty Arizona ranches were set loose in an exotic country with a few bucks and eager smiles.

Rich Egles was making the most of his sightseeing opportunities. "We were paid $9.00 and went off at 4:00 for liberty. I was able to leave the ship and headed for Paris. Got to see the Eiffel Tower, Arch de Triumphe, Louvre, Versailles Palace (which I really enjoyed), Cathedral of Notre Dame, and many other historic spots. I had a great time seeing this part of the world in the time we had to do it, and believe it or not, it did not include any girly shows." Rich did indeed get a good tour of the great culture before him, a notable accomplishment considering competing sites and peer pressure.

John Carmichael visited Paris with buddy Steve Carpenter and others, including a reserve lieutenant and professor from Penn State who was fluent in French. "He found us lodgings in a Left Bank pension," John recalled. "Steve and I shared a room with a balcony, the tariff was $1.50 per day. We ate in the garden, a lunch of filet mignon, French fries, and watercress salad, cost $1.00. A bottle of wine was fifty cents." But John and Steve did not sit idly in their room or only eat in the garden, they ventured forth into the streets and sights of the pre-war City of Light, "Our French-speaking shipmate led us to a huge department store and commandeered a saleslady to escort us throughout the store and help us with shopping. Afterwards, Steve and I felt confident enough to go sightseeing on our own. We stopped at a street-side restaurant. Steve spoke a bit of French but I did not. He left me at a table while he visited the men's room. A burly waiter asked me to order. The only thing I could think of was beer and apparently my version was close enough to his language that he took my order. We had a couple more then decided to visit the Louvre. Before long we needed to visit a restroom. The quest became urgent so we literally ran through the museum looking for a restroom. We held the world record for touring the Louvre-thirty minutes." At best, a couple of young American sailors in their dress whites, uncomfortably squirming and running through the hallowed halls of the Louvre, breezing by much of the greatest art in the world, must have presented the probably not so bemused French with an odd first impression of Americans.

Carmichael and Steve also visited a night club where the "waitresses were scantily clad, in shoes," and where they spotted the venerable Captain Wilson. They were most definitely in Paris, but it was pre-war France where many still remembered the devastation of WWI and now feared yet another war was in the foreseeable future. Carmichael observed that the people, outside of the raucous clubs, seemed slightly edgy and concerned at the very least. While back in Cherbourg, the sailors, in uniform with standard issue long raincoats, were walking in the light rain past some children playing in their yard. "When their mother saw us in uniform, she rushed out to gather up her kids yelling 'Allemand! Allemand' (German!)." No matter that the Americans did not resemble German army troops, having been severely bloodied several times before, the French no doubt feared and expected yet another German war.

Nashville was a new, beautiful, and powerful ship. Her sweeping, sleek design was not yet interrupted with anti-aircraft guns and radar that the coming war would necessitate. As she moved from exotic port to port in Europe, she was building an image of a glamour ship of sorts. Later, on a high profile trip to Rio de Janeiro, that image would be solidified. Nashville continued her Goodwill tour, visiting numerous ports including Stockhom and Gothenbur, Sweden and Gravesend, and Portsmouth, England.

In order to reach Stockholm, the Nashville had to carefully navigate a beautiful deep and narrow fjord, seemingly guarded on both sides by an assortment of colorful houses, providing the deck crew with yet another new and interesting postcard view. Seaman 2c W. Frank Gill was amused by what he saw while traversing the fjord. "We were passing one small cover after another and then there would be a boat livery or station with huge signs with this word 'FART;' this amused us sailors to no end." Knowing that "fart" roughly translated to "speed limit" would have lessened the humorous implication.

The ship anchored in Stockholm opposite the ornate Swedish Royal Palace, with a clear view of all of the government buildings from the decks. Within fifteen minutes of docking, thanks to arrangements made through the American Consul by supply officer Lieutenant Commander Charles F. House, over 400 kilos of fresh eggs were delivered and taken aboard. Infinitely better than the standard powdered variety, the crew was grateful. The new, sleek Nashville was quite an attraction, docked almost in the city center, her modern steel superstructure in sharp contrast to the heavy, older concrete buildings. There were so many curious visitors that came aboard during the initial open tour that she listed slightly to port and some visitors were gently moved to starboard side to correct the list. The first night Nashville was docked the Swedish Navy hosted an aquavit-drenched party for the crew at their officers' club. Aquavit and delicacies such as pickled herring were a first for many of the crew, many more comfortable with beer, whiskey, and hamburgers. Reviews were mixed at best, but they did greatly enjoy the festivities and hospitality of their guests, to say nothing of the effects of the aquavit.

The next adventure of the European tour was Gothensburg, Sweden, where, due to limited available dock space, the ship docked in the outer harbor, so she was not as much of an attraction for the locals. But despite the distance from the downtown area most of the crew made it into town to see a few attractions, including museums and restaurants. Some of the men had their first taste of caviar and were less than enthusiastic about the experience. But as always, they enjoyed the local color and hospitality of the Swedes and were beginning to appreciate the aquavit more and more.

From the frigid fjords and caviar of Sweden the crew next briefly saw the heather- covered blue hills and the golden sand beach of Weymouth, England before moving on to Portsmouth where Nashville docked close to historic HMS Victory, Admiral Nelson's flagship in the epic 1805 naval Battle of Trafalgar, when the British defeated a combined Spanish and French fleet. The graceful steel hull and decks of the modern Nashville towered over the stubby wooden little Victory, armed with more firepower and crew members than Admiral Nelson could ever have imagined on a single man of war.

While in Portsmouth, the Nashville was to receive a sealed packet of top secret information from the British on their sonar system. The Brits were continuing to woo the Americans as they wanted the assistance of the United States. Churchill was overtly and actively trying to build a personal relationship with President Roosevelt, something Roosevelt could appreciate on both a personal and political level. The British hosted a formal full dress uniform where all the medals would be shown reception for the Nashville. Great food, plentiful drink, and a common language and cultural roots made for quite an entertaining evening for everyone. Nashvillers and the British hosts were on the friendliest yet best behavior. But this was not all about good times and entertainment. Captain Wilson had been ordered to report to the American Ambassador in London where he was notified he was to take aboard $25 million (exactly $23,983,212 at the set exchange rate) in gold bullion from the Bank of England, for safe transport and delivery to the United States in New York. John Carmichael was part of the crew involved with taking possession of the gold. "On the portside of the ship, next to the wharf, the 20MM battery was manned, augmented by the Marines with machine guns, Browning automatics, and rifles. I was in charge of the unarmed loading party. Gazing at the firepower on the ship and visualizing an attack from shoreward, I noted that our party would be in the middle of any exchange of fire, unfavorable odds for our survival. When the shipment had not arrived by noon, the captain became increasingly concerned, for Nashville had to cross the bar before low water and the tide was ebbing. The shipment finally arrived in an unescorted, dilapidated old biscuit truck." Apparently the British had decided that the best security was to be totally mundane and travel unescorted as if it was nothing more than a biscuit truck doing what biscuit trucks do. It worked.

A cargo net was placed under the loading crane in the event any of the gold broke loose and plunged towards the water. Some sailors were given duty they would tell their grandchildren about, loading the individual boxes of gold bullion. Harold J. Landry remembers how "they loaded the gold by hand up the gangplank; they put the gold in the Powder Room (ammunition room) and put a lock on it. We had a lot of young (eighteen to twenty year olds) sailors move that gold." One of those young gold-carrying sailors was Plankie W. Frank Gill S2c. It was far more monetary wealth than any of them would ever accumulate during the lifetimes.

In all, the Nashville took on board 429 boxes of gold bars, with 214 boxes stored in Magazine A-511, and 215 boxes placed in Magazine A-512, and padlocked with keys given to Captain Wilson, and also placed in the safe of Supply Officer Lieutenant Commander C. F. House. Scuttlebutt had it that no one aboard Nashville had actually signed a document for the gold, acknowledging delivery and providing a receipt in kind. As it turns out, that scuttlebutt was true. England had just handed $23,000,000 of gold bullion to the crew of the USS Nashville and had no written proof of it. Her Majesty's treasury bureaucrats must have been aghast once they realized what had occurred. But it was too late, as the Nashville sailed on.

Laden with British gold and hospitality, Nashville departed Portsmouth and sailed onto the next port, Gravensend, England where Rich Egles, not quite eighteen years old, continued his personal tour of Europe. "I went ashore and visited a reserve airport at Gravesend, took in a movie, and returned to the ship. Our ship was probably the only American ship in the European area at that time. It was brand new so it did attract a lot of attention. Next day, since I had no money to spend, I thought I'd just walk around Gravesend, which is a small town. An English gentleman was standing in the middle of the road looking down the hill at our ship. As I approached him he asked if that was my ship. I said, 'of course sir, that's the USS Nashville.' We conversed somewhat and then he asked why I wasn't going to London. I told him I was financially embarrassed as I did my touring in the previous ports and was now broke. So he said, 'well, you are a guest in England,' and he was going to show me the sights in London."

The kindly gentlemen bought round trip tickets for Egles and a one way ticket for himself, as he was going home to London. Egles remembered how "he really showed me everything possible in the time allowed. I was bewildered with his thoughtfulness and generosity. As we walked the streets of London I would feel a tapping on my back. Pretty young girls passing by tapped the star on my collar and smiled. The gentlemen explained it was to do with one of their navy traditions going back to Admiral Nelson's day and it would bring good luck to the tapper. I don't know about the sailor. I got to see the Changing of the Guard, Big Ben, Westminster Abbey, London Bridge, and much more, ending up with dinner at a Piccadilly Circus restaurant. I thanked him wholeheartedly. I corresponded with this gentleman for quite some time, but after London was blitzed so thoroughly by Germany we lost contact." Whether the kind soul stopped writing of his own accord or perhaps more likely fell victim to Hitler's terror raids is unknown.

Nashville then departed England September 21 and endured more than the common fall stormy weather and high seas of the North Atlantic. Nashville ran straight into a full-fledged hurricane that tested both ship and crew. As Edward Fitzgerald said, "The ship was in the tail end of a hurricane that devastated the New England coast. The Nashville was tossed around in sixty to eighty feet waves like a toy in a bathtub. My duty station was at the helm and the aft steering behind the diesel engine underneath the aircraft deck, a very scary duty station for a twenty-year-old seaman since the vertical ladder to reach the station was always locked in conditions Able and Baker. However, the ship weathered the storm and I was able to return to my hometown of North Andover, Massachusetts for a visit."

Robert Shaffer did not fare so well, experiencing extreme seasickness and turning more shades of green than sold by Sherwin-Williams. "I was so seasick they locked me up in officer country, in the shower, and left me alone." There were far worse places to be left alone while desperately ill and being tossed about like a fishing float in rough seas. It was an ordeal for both crew and ship but both survived, albeit with some damage and injuries. The crew suffered a fair assortment of contusions, abrasions, broken bones, chipped teeth, and seasickness.

The first major order of duty for the crew upon Nashville docking at the New York Navy Yard was to safely and securely unload the British gold. At 0600 on October 4, and under heavy Marine guard, the seals were broken and the gold hand loaded on deck in four neat stacks. An order was received from the Federal Reserve Bank to "kindly deliver to a representative, Mr. D. J. Cameron, whose specimen signature appears below, the 429 boxes said to contain gold bars receive by you from the Bank of England at Portsmouth, England." The American reception of the gold was in bold contrast to the understated British style of delivering it in a biscuit truck. John Carmichael took note of the difference. "A convoy of armored trucks escorted by police cars and motorcycles, fire engines and ambulances. The noise was deafening with horns and sirens blasting and lights flashing. I don't know if the press covered our arrival but I feel certain that if any hijackers had aspiration for the gold, they would have been thwarted by traffic jams and hordes of pedestrians." The British approached the security issue by being discreet, understated, deceptive, and minimalist. The Americans approached the same challenge by being overt, forceful, bold, and grand. Both worked.

As always, sailors are glad to return to their home port, or any home-like port, and such was the case with the Nashville crew upon their return from Europe. GM Henry D. Van Wagner noted, "In Europe people seemed afraid of Hitler and what he was doing. The way things were going, I wished to be in any place except Europe." Well, they weren't in Europe now; they were in the great liberty port of New York City, after weeks of travel abroad. Firm land, great skyscrapers, theatre, girls, restaurants, museums, girls and more girls awaited them.

Nashville had docked in the Hudson River and it was but a healthy walk for the crew to visit Times Square and the rest of the sites of the city including, for some, the recently installed automatic doors at Pennsylvania Station, a new contraption unfamiliar to all but a few. Whatever the sites were to be seen, the pleasures to be enjoyed, the crew probably covered each and every one of them.

Nashville finally returned to Philadelphia on October 5, her shakedown and goodwill cruise to Europe highly successful but not entirely uneventful. Rich Egles AM2C remembers, "There was a fire discovered in the hanger one afternoon. One plane was damaged by a bomb going off accidentally while at Delaware Capes early on. The next incident was a fire on one of the planes, but no damage was done. There was a little trouble in the engine room when we left Portsmouth. We couldn't make a speed run of thirty knots as a result, but that was fixed. Basically all went well on the cruise, ship-wise." In Philadelphia, like in most ports, the crew painted, cleaned the decks, and at times scrapped barnacles when possible. They also had liberty of course, and many took the 13th Street streetcar downtown to see the sites. The Goodwill tour was over, Nashville and crew not only survived but comported themselves well. More tests and tribulations were coming their way, but the rite of full passage into the US Navy active fleet was complete and secure.

CHAPTER 2
Good Times: Bad Beginning

***

"I went to investigate the source of this miracle and found two bottles of Scotch amidst the bandsmen."
-John Carmichael

***

On January 5, 1939 Nashville arrived in Norfolk, Virginia to take on provisions and then sailed onto various ports in the Caribbean including Guantanamo, Trinidad, and Panama for routine fleet battle exercises before returning to Norfolk on April 1. After a brief routine stint at the Philadelphia Navy Yard she sailed to New York and anchored once again in the Hudson for the opening of the 1939 World's Fair. Several dozen ships, far fewer than originally planned, were to participate in the ceremonies and activities. The ships sailed through the humid Narrows at 0530 April 29th to assigned moorings, led by four old destroyers closely followed by the new light cruisers including Nashville, then battleship USS Texas BB-24, newer destroyers, the carrier Ranger CV-4, carrier tender Langley AV3, and then submarines and auxiliary vessels. Nashville and the other large ships moored in the Hudson River while the smaller, shallower draft ships moored dockside. The ships were open to the public and it was estimated that over 50,000 people would tour them. As guests of President Roosevelt aboard the Presidential Yacht Potomac AG-25, the Crown Prince and Princess of Denmark reviewed the fleet. It was a major event not only for New York and the participants of the Fair, but also for the US Navy and the nation itself, still recovering from the Depression and increasingly wary of the troubling news in Europe and China ignited by German and Japanese nationalism and militarism.

The City of New York hosted a formal banquet for the officers of the ships. The embossed invitation read in part: "Officers and their bona fide wives are invited." As it was, the officers were all seated at tables on the ballroom floor while their "bona fide" wives were relegated to the encircling balcony. While not invited to the formal banquet, the Nashville crew however was given free tickets to the Fair, quite a memorable experience for all. Seaman 2c W Frank Gill was assigned to the parade detail but switched with another crewman to operate the search lights. "We were operating the lights moving from side to side and up and down. We let the lights swing down on the row of buildings across the river and soon got orders from the Admiral to 'get those lights off of those apartments.'" New York was quite the liberty town for the crew as they visited Rockefeller Center, the Empire State Building, saw Sonia Hennie and Lowel Thomas, and a host of other celebrities and sites. While war may have been on the distant horizon for America, Nashville and crew were still operating in a peacetime navy with peacetime rules and entertainment.

Crewman Rich Egles enjoyed himself at the Fair, "there were lots of ships in the harbor and visitors were allowed on board. That was always an interesting time, especially when the young gals would show up. During my school days I didn't date girls, go to proms, or any of that stuff. My Navy days were broadening my interests." Indeed they were for Egles and many other teens aboard Nashville. Egles said, "This brings to mind three girls that came aboard. It looked as though they were unhappy and arguing with each other. So, as the goodwill ambassador I was supposed to be, I asked what their problem was. It seems they took a launch out to the wrong ship. They wanted to go to the USS Brooklyn to see a Marine they had met previously. I told them this turned out to be the luckiest day of their lives, I would be their escort for the afternoon and show them most anything and everything they wanted to see on the ship. As it turned out, one of the girls lived very close to my Aunt Lena in the Bronx. We struck up a friendship and Millie wrote letters to me for years while I was the lonely sailor out to sea." More than a few pen pals were created at the World's Fair.

At the conclusion of her Fair duties Nashville got underway on April 29 for her first South American trip. Nashville had become a high profile ship in her short life and was increasingly seen as a "glamour ship" among others in the Navy, and now she carried both Admiral King, Commander in Chief US Fleet, and General George Marshall, Army Chief of Staff, along with their respective staffs to yet another exotic port. Docking briefly at San Juan, Puerto Rico to disembark a sailor that had been electrocuted while cleaning under a generator, and then at Trinidad on her way to Rio de Janeiro for the Pan American Defense Conference, she soon arrived in Rio de Janeiro. The pompous Italian Dictator Benito Mussolini had previously dispatched his daughter Edda to Brazil in order to persuade fellow Dictator Getulio Vargas to consider joining the Axis powers. America did not look kindly on such a potential arrangement in her own hemisphere, in direct conflict with the Monroe Doctrine. Hence, much of the purpose of the Nashville trip with the aforementioned dignitaries. Nashville finally arrived and docked at the main docks near the center of the city on May 25 and stayed in Rio for a little over two socially active and culturally educational weeks.

The ship's Shore Patrol (SP) was organized into two sections in order for everyone to get some real liberty. Some of the smarter men, like John Carmichael, opted for the first SP duty so as to better know what to do and where to go when their own liberty commenced. As part of the first SP group, Carmichael and the senior patrol officer were quartered in a luxury hotel in connecting rooms with balconies for the sum price of $3.50 with an extra ten cents for room service breakfast. It was not bad duty for cruiser sailors. A car and driver was also supplied and provided another cultural lesson. "My driver was quite wild, charging about as if he was in a tank," said John Carmichael. "He gave me a Brazilian drivers'-ed course: the first car to enter an intersection had the right of way, a very hazardous policy, and vehicular traffic had the right of way over pedestrians. I witnessed a car bump a lady who was not seriously hurt, and as he drove by he shook his fist at her for getting in his way." John found the SP duty educational at times. "I am not a prude but I was shocked at the depth of human decadence." Nevertheless, liberty was enjoyable for John and everyone else. Many prominent Brazilians invited officers into their homes and John was with a group of officers hosted at a 3,000 acre orange plantation complete with swimming pool where they were served a drink none had had before, "The cocktail was a powerful concoction made from a sugarcane, it was only slightly less lethal than Lucrezia Borgia's 'social' wine used in assisted deaths."

But that was not the end of the adventures for John Carmichael and the crew. The Rio de Janeiro English Speaking Society had invited 125 enlisted men to a party at an exclusive country club and John was the officer assigned to be in charge of the men. Upon arriving at the club in his crisp dress whites, he immediately noticed that "the young ladies were prettier and more jovial than those at officers' parties." The evening's musical entertainment was provided by the talented Nashville band. But at first that talent did not manifest itself as the musicians did not quite jell together, but well into the evening they started sounding better and better. "I went to investigate the source of this miracle," said John, "and found two bottles of Scotch amidst the bandsmen." Sailors or not, musicians are musicians. Apparently the booze had been put there by the local Standard Oil executive who was also the president of the English Speaking Society. He certainly understood more than simply English.

However, not all was lubricated as smoothly for the party. One of the party sponsors, a very attractive middle-aged woman, approached Carmichael, and in her perfectly enunciated if somewhat nasal English proclaimed, "This is a terrible party!" When John inquired as to why she thought so she replied, "We ladies went to a great deal of trouble preparing a fine buffet and the sailors are not eating anything. They are all at the bar drinking." John told her he would take care of the situation, and he certainly did. "Gathering some of the leaders, I gave the following orders: 'The bar is closed. Go into the food room and consume all the food, then the bar will be reopened.'"

Sailors can be highly intelligent and able to consume massive quantities of both food and alcohol with an uncanny ability to prioritize the obvious and if ordered. The entire lot of them took John's order to heart and quickly completed their mission. "About thirty minutes later the food was gone and I reopened the bar." The ladies were happy and the party continued. Under the circumstance and environment one would think that the crew would be at least a little bit wild and rambunctious, but not so according to John. "Our sailors' conduct was a credit to the Navy. Only one old rummy became a bit pixilated and was returned to the ship in the paddy wagon and put to bed."

The parties and ceremonies continued with General Marshall hosting a smaller party for notable Brazilians on the forecastle of Nashville.

The Brazilian government also held a large ball for the crew, with the prerequisite women, wine, food, and diplomatic courtesies. The Nashville had fully become, as Seaman and Plankie Walter Benson stated, "a glamour ship." Nashville, after days and days of seemingly endless parties, balls, and officious events, carrying a few Brazilian VIPs, and having left a great impression on politicians, businessmen, cultural mavens, and the local girls, finally departed and steamed to Annapolis, arriving June 20. After a short period of hosted events at the venerable naval academy, the ship then made her way down the coast to Norfolk, where she took on provisions and conducted routine maintenance in preparation for her next duty assignment in the Pacific. Fully requisitioned, she departed Norfolk and transited the Panama Canal on a hot and oppressively humid June 23, arriving at San Pedro, California on July 16.

For several weeks the Nashville operated with the Pacific Fleet on intense training maneuvers off the coast of Southern California. Gunnery practice, anti-aircraft gunnery, anti-submarine evasion, invasion formations, and just about everything else the Navy can do was practiced. And for good reason as German saber-rattling in Europe intensified and the Japanese war machine continued to grind up Chinese civilians and military alike.

Having finished training maneuvers with excellent marks, in August Nashville turned to starboard and headed north to San Francisco. On a clear and warm August day Nashville cut through the swirling waters under the Golden Gate Bridge, turned to port, and sailed past Angel Island, at one time the pristine west coast version of Ellis Island, and docked at Mare Island, at the northern part of San Francisco Bay. Sailors yet again got busy scrapping barnacles and painting as usual. But the crew also got to visit the nearby International Exposition on man-made Treasure Island in the middle of San Francisco Bay, where no doubt some saw Sally Rand slowly reveal herself and other cultural treasures along with the famous 'China Clipper' fleet, tied up on the eastern side of the island. The next stop was Portland, Oregon for Navy Day festivities. Nashville slowly sailed up the Columbia River and docked close to the battleship USS Oregon. After the local events and tours, Nashville returned to fleet maneuvers off idyllic Santa Barbara in southern California. For the crew, it was a routine life of touring, chipping paint, painting, liberty, and patrol exercises that had become quite comfortable and familiar as the new ship slowly found her rhythm in the peacetime Navy.

In early April 1940, Nashville once again crossed the Pacific and visited Hawaii, docking off of LaHaina, Maui where the crew had a few days liberty among the lush island beauty, town bars and dives, and houses of pleasure before setting course for nearby Honolulu. Approaching Oahu the ship docked directly under the Aloha Tower in Honolulu, the first warship to ever have that honor. Not one to stay in any port very long, in mid-April Nashville departed Honolulu and set a course back to Mare Island with high ranking naval officials and families on board, including Secretary of the Navy Edison and Admiral King. As soon as she arrived at Mare Island she was put into dry-dock for routine maintenance and repairs, including the proverbial barnacle scrapping, rumored to have traveled over 1,000,000 nautical miles during her brief life.

Late September 1940 Nashville once again returned to the warm blue waters of Pearl Harbor, operating for a few months with the Hawaii based fleet. She then did a quick return trip to California and just as quickly returned again to Pearl Harbor before the end of the year. Both ship and crew were piling up the sea miles and fleet experience that would serve them well during the war. Constant training and drills kept the crew as well honed and disciplined as any in the navy. Fire control was so good that Nashville earned the right to paint a big white "E" on her smokestack indicating "Excellence in Gunnery" with a white hash mark indicating "Best Light Cruiser in Class" to boot. As Richard Egles now knew, "The USS Nashville required you to be the best of the best." And they were and would continue to be during the war to come. The crew received prize money for their gunnery performance.

Expert naval gunnery achievements by Nashville notwithstanding, the combined military power of the Unites States at this time, in a world already a year into a war that would explode in magnitude and horror, was an unbelievable fourteenth. Besides the obvious, Germany, France, and Britain, other military powers surpassing the Americans were Russia, Italy, Japan, China, Belgium, Netherlands, Portugal, Spain, Sweden, and Switzerland. To be sure, the American Navy was not fourteenth, a critical fact that would be of great significance early during the coming war to hold back the Axis while America ramped up production, training and military power the likes of which the world had never witnessed. But America was unprepared and vulnerable. New ships like the Nashville, manned by well trained and disciplined crews, were valuable and far too rare.

In February 1941 Nashville, along with three other cruisers, departed Pearl Harbor and transported a contingent of brave but ultimately unlucky Marines to soon-to-be ill-fated Wake Island. No one could have foreseen at the time what impact on American morale this small group of men, along with a group of construction workers, would have in their future-determined defense of Wake Island and the famous telegram that rallied a somber and beleaguered nation. No matter that "Send us more Japs" was the beginning and ending of a telegram, not the message itself. It exemplified the fighting spirit of the Marine bulldogs and civilian construction workers that held Wake Island for some time against overwhelming odds, only to be eventually overwhelmed, beheaded, tortured, and otherwise abused by their Japanese captors.

For several more months Nashville continued to be based at Pearl Harbor and was an integral part of fleet training, maneuvers, and gunnery practice. One such practice was near Midway Island and provided inadvertent entertainment and lore for the crew. Coxswain W. Frank Gill saw that "the first lieutenant started out with the towed targets in a forty-foot launch to place the targets about 500 yards out when we saw him waving his arms frantically. The coxswain had forgotten to put the boat plug in and they were taking water in fast." Imagine the embarrassment for a young lieutenant, in full view of his own ship and crew and most of the Pacific Fleet, sinking on his first command, on a Launch at that. Gill noted, "Fortunately, they were able to get back alongside with a boat full of water and we managed to haul them in." It could have been worse and no doubt the lieutenant's fellow officers rode him mercilessly for it.

In May 1941 Nashville and a substantial part of the Pacific Fleet stationed at Hawaii were officially transferred to the Atlantic Fleet to assist with Lend-Lease, show the flag in the increasingly war-active Atlantic, and for unspecified duty. During May, June, and July, fully 25% of the entire Pacific Fleet passed through the Panama Canal into the Atlantic. Events and circumstances were slowly heating up. On May 21 in the South Atlantic, the US freighter Robin Moor was torpedoed and sunk by the German submarine U-69, but all eight passengers and the unsuspecting crew of thirty-five survived. Relations between and the US and Germany were further strained.

The transfer orders to the Atlantic Fleet were secret and not even the ship's commanding officers knew their destinations upon departing Pearl

Harbor. Opening the sealed orders after they left Pearl and were well out to sea, they discovered they were to traverse the Panama Canal at night (for secrecy reasons) and join the Atlantic Fleet. Ultimately these orders saved the ships from the infamous Japanese attack on Pearl Harbor. Such is fate in war. The Nashville, light cruisers Brooklyn, Philadelphia, and Savannah, two destroyer squadrons, the old battleships Mississippi, New Mexico, and Idaho, and the carrier Yorktown were doing serious patrol duty in the Atlantic by the end of May. At this time the United States Navy still lacked modern battleships, with the USS Virginia BB-48 commissioned in 1923 as the Navy's newest fully-active battleship. Most of the ships that would fight WWII were still on the drawing boards. Even the newly commissioned battleships USS Washington BB-56 and USS North Carolina BB-55 had yet to finish shakedown cruises and were not yet available for intense fleet duty.

After weeks of sea duty, Nashville docked in Boston on June 19 where most of the crew was granted liberty. Delbert Ford SF2c had a different than the usual sailor on liberty in Boston experience. "Some of us Nashvillers went to Fenway Park to take in the Boston Red Sox and St. Louis Browns game. Before the game Tom Cruise and I went down to the St. Louis dugout and asked if we could take a picture. The manager said yes and asked where we were from. Tom answered first and said Texas and the manager told the Texans to come out, and a couple did. We took their picture. Then he asked me, and I told him California and he said for the California players to come out, and a lot of them did. It started to rain during the game and a few Nashville sailors were sitting below us, and instead of going undercover somewhere they picked up empty chairs and put them over their heads to keep dry till the rain stopped. The next day in a Boston paper they had a cartoon of us doing these things around a drawing of one of the Boston players." The world at war was fast approaching but there was still time for baseball.

The British had received permission from the Free Danish Government-in-Exile (London) to occupy Iceland, strategically located for transatlantic shipping. But Winston Churchill needed every man he could get for combat duty in North Africa so he made a request to President Roosevelt to establish an American garrison at a minimum in Iceland to relieve British troops. At the time American draftees could not be legally stationed outside of American territories so the all-volunteer Marines were picked for the assignment. The Marines had in fact been transferred from the Pacific to the Atlantic with the ships in May. With the orders "In cooperation with the British garrison, defend Iceland against hostile attack," a Marine brigade on four transports, an oil tanker, and two cargo ships, escorted by the Nashville, Brooklyn, New York, and Arkansas, along with thirteen destroyers sailed for Reykjavik, Iceland. Marine Raymond D. Chaney CWO4 was on an old converted four-stack destroyer troopship transport on his way to Bermuda to join the Nashville crew, but the ship had departed too quickly and Raymond had to return to Norfolk and then Boston before he was able to catch up with the elusive Nashville.

While officially neutral, the United States was in fact helping the British via Lend-Lease and joint intelligence. The Germans were bidding their time for war with America, putting forth effort to avoid directly provoking the Americans until a later, more advantageous date. But in the fog of war the unanticipated and undesired are inevitable, and such it was with duty in the Atlantic for Nashville and the United States Navy. Since April 18, when Admiral King's Operation Plan 3-41 was implemented, Nashville and the US Navy had been working under much different rules of engagement than prior, and certainly much different than was generally understood by the public. The previous rules of engagement accepted, if not officially, well-understood lines of demarcation of the Western Hemisphere, and placed the Axis powers on notice that any incursion, including but not limited to tracking and attacking British ships, both merchant and navy, would be unacceptable and considered an act of war against the United States. Specifically, Admiral King's new orders were: "If any such naval vessels or aircraft are encountered within twenty-five miles of Western Hemisphere territory, except the Azores, warn them to move twenty-five miles from such territory and, in case of failure to heed such warning, attack them." There would be no defensive waiting for attacks on British ships. Long before Pearl Harbor, the US Navy was in a shooting war.

Nashville returned to Hampton Roads July 24, 1941 and took on provisions while the crew had liberty where Bob Shafer remembers a crewman commandeering a horse, although he had never been on one before, and both man and horse getting bloody noses as they fell and slid across the street, and others carousing in rickshaw-like bicycles in a most hazardous but entertaining manner. After provisioning, Nashville sailed for New York.

Like scores of years of sailors before him, Albert L. Pender MM1c enjoyed his liberty. In America's largest city he simply got drunk. "Not proud of it, but I got drunk in New York City and woke up in Harlem on a Saturday night. I didn't know how I got there." It is unlikely his experience was not repeated by others who had spent a long time at sea. Sometimes roll call the morning after the first night of liberty could be interesting. Lawrence Spence, who was not only a diver, an incredibly dangerous job in those days, but also ran the captain's launch, a fitting job for someone whose father was a lobsterman, would do roll call. Sometimes a sailor or two bordered on being green, other times one could see they were simply in pain. When he came to the "Bs" he always bellowed out George Bustin's full name, "George Leland Joseph Bustin," and Bustin would consistently respond, "here, here, here, and here!" in a running dialogue they kept up for their time aboard the Nashville. Later, one of Spencer's secret projects was the air ventilation system he rigged up for the diver's locker room. When the war started, Nashville still had a great multitude of portholes that almost gave the young ship a luxury ocean liner appearance if one looked at the sides of the ship below the main deck. But these would be liabilities during combat and had to be welded shut to keep water from pouring in and light from beaming out. Spence managed to make two portholes that fed into the diver's locker room look just like they were welded shut when, in fact, there was a small hole to insert an Allen wrench that opened them a bit, feeding welcome fresh sea air into the room. It was an effective plan. During numerous inspections the officers never discovered this ingenious deception, except for the brilliant thirty-year-old Len Meyer, who first hinted to Spence and others during the 2005 Nashville reunion, some sixty-four years later, that he was aware of the ruse and let it slip for the benefit of the men.

Leaving New York, the ship's next base of operations was once again Bermuda, a lovely set of islands 570 miles into the Atlantic off the North Carolina coast, arriving there August 20 and docking at Hamilton, the largest city. But Nashville arrived without one of her crew, Allan D. Ensor. "While moored in New York I requested six days leave. Upon my return I could not find Nashville so reported aboard the USS Hornet (CV-8). 'You are twenty-four hours AWOL' the Quartermaster of the

Watch told me as he examined my leave papers. 'You were due back 0700 yesterday.' Three days later I was aboard the fleet oiler USS Cimmaron (AO-22) heading for Bermuda. 'Thirty days restriction' was the Skipper's order, 'to begin the day you reported to the Hornet.' I simply had not read my leave papers." Allan always carefully read them thereafter.

Most of her Bermuda time was increasingly tense Neutrality Patrols in the Central Atlantic including a purported search patrol for the famed German Cruiser Prince Eugene. If Nashville was in fact searching for the German cruiser, one wonders what would have occurred considering Admiral King's orders. Nashville may well have been the instigator of the first major American naval action of WWII. Fortunately, the question remains a history "what if" exercise at best and the ship continued operations, albeit tense at times, in peace.

On September 1, 1941 in Operation Plan 7-41, Admiral King laid out expectations and policies regarding engaging Axis vessels in hostile acts based on President Roosevelt's letter to Admiral Stark on revised rules of engagement. This plan for US Navy vessels stated, "Destroy hostile forces that threaten shipping." It was clearly understood what and who constituted hostile forces. It was but four days later that the German submarine U-552 fired a deadly spread of torpedoes at destroyer USS Greer DD-145, barely missing, as did the return depth charges of the Greer. As a result, Plan 7B-41 was implemented on September 22 with the clear and blunt orders for Nashville and the Atlantic Fleet in regards to any meeting with a German or Italian vessel. "The vessel may not be stopped and boarded. If there is conclusive evidence that she is a combatant naval vessel, either merchant type raider or a regular naval vessel, she shall be destroyed. Operate as under war conditions, including complete darkening of ships when at sea east of longitude sixty degrees west." Nashville was in a hot zone. The peacetime Navy, at least in the Atlantic, was a thing of the past and America was closer to war than the public could possibly imagine. In October the brand new destroyer USS Kearny DD-432 was hit by two torpedoes from U-56 and suffered eleven dead, America's first casualties. Admiral King replied, "Whether the country knows it or not, we are at war." The families of the dead sailors certainly knew it.

During Thanksgiving the Nashville crew was invited to be guests aboard the carrier USS Wasp for an evening of "smokers," the popular night at the movies aboard all Navy ships, enjoyed by thousands of sailors in a respite from constant chores and routine. It was to be the very last such evening for the Nashville crew.

The Nashville was swinging around the hook in Grassy Bay, Bermuda on December 7, 1941 when she got word of the Japanese attack on Pearl Harbor. "We sent SPs ashore to round up our crew in Hamilton. We were all in shock but had expected war to start any day," said Patrick Carigan FC3c. Indeed, war itself was not that much of a surprise, but the audacious attack and resultant catastrophic damage to the Pacific Fleet was a shocker for everyone.

Robert L. Shafer BM2c had a common reaction. "At first I could not believe it, and then I got mad and was happy when we got underway the next day because I knew we were headed for a chance to pay them back." Richard A. Egles was on board that Sunday morning, "I became very excited and disturbed that this could happen." He instinctively knew the crew and country "had a tough brutal job ahead of us."

Men who had yet to board Nashville, many yet to join the Navy, and some yet, still in high school, remembered that moment also. Elvin Crockett was a teenager hunting rabbits in Kansas when he heard the news. He learned to hate the Japanese quickly, a neighbor, only two years older, is still interred in the Arizona. Newlyweds Albert and Betty Gaines were lying on the living room floor of their new home in Englewood, Colorado, relaxing and reading the Sunday Denver Post when they heard the news on the radio. Albert of course, like millions of Americans, could have no idea how that treacherous event would impact their lives, how they would sacrifice, fight, and see horrible things never imagined.

Quickly, those on liberty were rounded up by the Shore Patrol or heard the news and raced by foot, bicycle, car, or taxi back to the ship. Even as the last men were running down the dock to board her, Nashville was casting off and making full steam for Casco Bay, Maine, arriving December 10. After provisioning and inspection, and awaiting a convoy, she departed Casco Bay on December 14, rendezvoused with the convoy, and escorted troops and cargo ships to Iceland via Halifax. This was not as simple or mundane as it sounds. Convoy duty in the stormy North Atlantic in December was anything but pleasurable. Alex Ensor BM1c thought it was "A nightmare. When steering Nashville I was constantly rocking back and forth from one leg to the other trying to maintain the stated course as the compass swung in both directions. Sleeping at night was impossible and several times I came out of my bunk when I thought Nashville would roll over on her side. There were times also when Nashville's outboard screws would appear completely out of the water. Lifelines were rigged inboard for safety but in spite of the extra precautions we lost a man over the side. A destroyer made a search but the body was not recovered." In the icy waters, the sailor most likely soon died of hypothermia even if he had a life vest on when he was swept over the side.

It was not any easier for the pilots of the ship's scout planes who had to be aloft whenever possible to help guard against German U-Boats. Buffeted by fierce crosswinds, bone-chilling temperatures, and low visibility, flying was not for the fainthearted and battered both man and plane. Landing was even riskier than flying. The planes needed to land in manageably smooth water; after all, they were simply planes with floats on the wings, not boats. Since the North Atlantic was far more likely to be choppy if not downright stormy, nature needed help to create a placid surface. The procedure was for the ship to make a wake, mitigating most of the waves and swells momentarily, and the pilot had to land promptly before the wake dissipated and then be picked up by the ship's crane. Off Greenland, once the wake dissipated too quickly and the pilot had his wing float violently ripped off by a wave and then the plane flipped over, completely upside down. Fortunately, and due to rapid work of the crew, the pilot was picked up quickly, wet and cold, but safe. Otherwise he would have been lost to hypothermia in the artic conditions.

Nashville repeated the Maine to Iceland roundtrip and finally returned to Hampton Roads on January 3, 1942. With men and material being hurriedly shipped about the Atlantic, Nashville was in demand and constantly on the go. Further escort duty took her to New York, Hampton Roads, and back to Bermuda. While steaming to Bermuda, Nashville rendezvoused with a destroyer escort. Allan Ensor BM1c requested the hull number from the signal bridge and when he was told it was '404' he knew it was the USS Rhind, the ship of his brother Ben. "Later, after both ships anchored in Bermuda, Ben came aboard Nashville in an official capacity as guard mail Petty Officer. He was a Fire Controlman 2c and we had a chance for a short visit. It would be the first of two times that our courses would cross during WWII." It would not be the last time brothers and even childhood friends of the Nashville crew crossed paths during the war.

Nashville arrived back at the Boston Navy Yard February 11 where the ship took on provisions and the crew had liberty. Marine Corporal Don R. Hill remembers how one sailor in particular seemed to have had an interesting and probably enjoyable time in Boston. "It was cold in Boston and I saw a naked sailor jump from a taxi in the middle of the night and run across the gangway." He of course smartly, if hurriedly, saluted the colors per regulation prior to stepping aboard. Departing Boston on March 4, Nashville then started the long journey to the Pacific and into history.

CHAPTER 3
The Halsey-Doolittle Raid: Shoot, Sink, and Rescue

***

"Instead of whistling a tune of Glenn Miller's popular at the time, you suddenly started thinking "Nearer My God to Thee."
-Francis Crawford

***

America needed a victory, badly. In early April 1942 the oil-soaked waters of Pearl Harbor contained the carcasses of the old backbone of the pacific fleet, the battleships Arizona, West Virginia, Oklahoma, Tennessee, and Nevada still resting on their muddy bottoms, the final resting place for over 1,102 in the case of the Arizona. Wake Island's overwhelmed and undersupplied marines had surrendered, Guam had fallen, the beleaguered and starving American and Filipino troops on Bataan had surrendered as had American forces in Manila and Luzon, McArthur had fled the Philippines, and Japanese forces had invaded Burma, the Solomon Islands, and Singapore and had launched attacks on Port Moresby in Australia. The British navy had been entirely swept from the Pacific, America lacked even one fully operational seasoned battleship, and the Japanese had lost nothing more significant than a destroyer. America and her Pacific Allies remained overwhelmingly outmanned and outgunned before a seemingly unstoppable and superhuman Japanese tsunami of military might. To achieve all of this the Japanese sacrifice was 15,000 killed and wounded. In return they achieved an outer defense territory stretching over 6,000 miles and had killed, wounded, and captured over 320,000 Allied soldiers, marines, airmen, and sailors. The Pacific Ocean covered more of the planet than all the land masses combined, and the Japanese controlled most of it. The Nashville, as part of secret Task Force 16 was about to attempt a symbolic but dangerous mission to give America its first victory. The sleeping giant Japanese Admiral Isoroku Yamamoto had warned of was in fact restlessly stirring awake.

Quietly, with neither pomp ceremony nor notice, the Nashville departed the Boston Navy Yard March 1, 1942 and sailed through the placid waters of the Cape Cod Canal on the way to New York for a short stay. Under great secrecy, she slipped out of New York on March 4 and trailed on course and then met up with the carrier USS Hornet (CV-8) which had left Norfolk that same day with equal stealth. Nashville, Hornet, and escorts joined a convoy of ships destined for Guadalcanal and Australia and passed through the heavily guarded Panama Canal where the convoy bid farewell and headed across the Pacific. For the young Nashville crew, it was an exciting but tense experience. Seasickness did not help and seemed to hit the new men particularly hard. Alex Zdurne was one of them. "I was so sick I thought I was going to die," said Zdurne. For new and more experienced crew alike, early war nerves and apprehension were evident. A couple of days out from Panama, Nashville and other task force ships picked up surface signals that appeared to be a submarine. Was this to be the first combat test of Nashville and her crew? Tense, alert, and determined, the crew was ready to take on the Japanese navy. All ships went to battle stations while the bobbing destroyers cut through the water at full steam to the contact point where they discovered the submarine to be a large sea turtle sunning on the surface, topped by a seagull. Both were lucky they were not depth-charged. Nashville's first combat experience would come later against a more formidable entity.

The task force stopped at San Diego on March 20 for additional provisions and a short liberty for some of the crew. During March 23-26, exercises were conducted off the coast of San Diego and of course the scuttlebutt was rampant. Still, only a few men other than the task force commander, Admiral Mitscher, knew what the real deal was at the time. Nashville and Hornet once again left a base quietly and sailed up the blacked out California coast. Sailing under the fog-wrapped towers of the Golden Gate Bridge on March 28, the Nashville turned north for the Mare Island Naval Base at the northernmost part of San Francisco Bay and the Hornet continued straight under the Oakland-San Francisco Bay Bridge to the Alameda Naval Base just south of the bridge where she had to cut through the mud of a partially dredged channel to dock.

As Nashville passed under the Golden Gate Bridge and cut through the cold swirling waters of San Francisco Bay, sailors could not only see San Francisco, they could smell it. Along the Embarcadero the roasting of MJB Coffee mixed with baking Boudin Sourdough bread and the salty air to create a unique San Francisco aroma. But no one aboard was going to see firsthand one of the world's greatest liberty ports, not on this voyage. And that included GM3c George Bustin who had not been home to nearby Oakland for over a year. It would be even longer and many thousands of sea miles before he got home to see his mother and three sisters (but not his three brothers in the Army, Army Air Force, and Merchant Marine).

Nashville turned to port at Angel Island, soon to be a center for German and Italian POWs, and headed up the channel to the naval base at Mare Island in Vallejo. The stay at Mare Island would be frantic, tense, and brief.

Doolittle's men and their planes had previously arrived at McClellan Field in Sacramento and then continued training at a suitably small airfield near the dusty, remote valley town of Willows, near Sacramento. It was not without notice by Doolittle's crews that it was April Fool's Day when they departed hot and flat Willows for the next leg of their mission, Alameda Naval Base in San Francisco Bay. After landing at Alameda the B-25s were carefully but quickly loaded onto the deck of the aircraft carrier, USS Hornet, in precise eight rows of two.

Bombers of this size had never seen the deck of an aircraft carrier in such numbers. And neither had the crew of an aircraft carrier seen such a massive display of bombers. At 1500 that afternoon the Hornet slowly pulled away from the Alameda dock, steamed a few miles north just past the Oakland-San Francisco Bay Bridge, and dropped anchor off Treasure Island for the night.

Bursting with assorted munitions and fuel, Nashville, one of the navy's newest cruisers, Hornet, the navy's newest aircraft carrier, and several support and screening ships departed foggy San Francisco Bay as Task Force 18 mid-morning on April 2, 1942, led by submarines Thresher and Trout with orders to sink any ship sighted en-route to still smoldering Pearl Harbor, to rendezvous with and become part of Task Force 16 already in Hawaii.

None of the men and few of the officers knew the destination and mission of Task Force 18. The Navy being the Navy, scuttlebutt, that ever-present, unofficial, and occasionally correct network of rumors, hopes, and fears went into high gear with one story starting at the bow of the ship and spreading to the stern and above to the gun directors and below to the engine room as others started in the stern and did the reverse. As Francis Crawford FC2c understatedly and succinctly said, "There's a lot of scuttlebutt that slips around from one person to another." Indeed. Most of the stories had the task force steaming to Pearl Harbor to reinforce what was left of the crippled Pacific fleet while others had Australia as a point of reinforcement and still others the Aleutians or even a Russian base at Kamchatka. None came close to discerning the true brilliance of the mission.

When the Nashville steamed under the majestic Golden Gate Bridge and out of San Francisco Bay the canvas covered ten-ton B-25s lashed to the deck of the Hornet were clearly visible and fueled further speculation that the mission was to reinforce Midway Island. Never in their wildest dreams and fears did the actual mission manifest itself. And just as well as the men would have had ample reason to doubt the sanity of their leaders and their own chances of survival. As Francis Crawford stated, "We woke up one morning and looked out there and there were cruisers and destroyers and an aircraft carrier with B-25s on it. Now, anybody in his right mind knows you can't fly those off that carrier so we must be going to Wake or Midway. We knew something was up as we seemed to be going in the wrong direction awfully quickly. When the old man came on and told us what we were going to do, that made your breath run cold. We had nothing out there. All our muscle was lying on the bottom of Pearl Harbor. How were we going to pull this off? Instead of whistling a tune of Glenn Miller's popular at the time, you suddenly started thinking "Nearer My God to Thee."

Past the Golden Gate Bridge a lighter than airship, commonly referred to as a dirigible, approached the Nashville from the stern, hovered over the hanger deck, and dropped a leather briefcase onto the fantail deck, very near Joe Fales. An anxious young officer grabbed the briefcase and hurried to the bridge, handing the package to the captain. Shortly thereafter, Captain Craven made the ship-wide announcement that they were going to bomb Tokyo and the crew responded with robust cheers throughout the ship. Joe Fales felt "a thrill over me that was almost overwhelming, I don't think I've been that thrilled since then." Simultaneously Nashville received Captain Mitscher's PS announcement on Hornet via semaphore: *The target of this task force is Tokyo. The Army is going to bomb Japan, and we're going to get them as close to the enemy as we can. This is a chance for all of us to give the Japs a dose of their own medicine.* "I was seventeen years old," said Samuel Sanders, who manned one of the 20mm anti-aircraft guns. "I was very gung-ho. I was very happy that we were going in to Japan to pay them back for what they did to Pearl Harbor; the crew was excited because they all had revenge for Pearl Harbor on their minds."

Perhaps part of their optimism was due to Captain Craven himself. An immensely popular Captain who could trace his naval heritage back to the Revolutionary War, who often ate in the mess hall with his men, he instilled confidence and loyalty. When Robert Jarvis had just come aboard, on one of his first days, he was cleaning the deck and he dropped the bucket, covering his dungarees with slop water, and just then he heard a marine yell, "Gangway," so he snapped to attention, slopped and soaked jeans and all. The beloved Captain Craven snapped, "Good morning, Seaman," and smartly saluted him. Jarvis swelled with pride and snapped off a return salute. He suddenly felt like a real sailor on a real ship, a part of the crew. Seventeen-year-old Jarvis said, "Captain Craven was such a great guy. At that moment, I became a real sailor."

The most unusual event of the trip to Hawaii occurred early with the appearance of Navy Blimp L-8. Blimp L-8, in a first for the Navy, maintained position just over the flight deck of the Hornet and lowered two swinging crates of navigator domes for the B-25 Mitchell bombers. While the fog cleared just past the Golden Gate, as it usually does, the blue skies did not last. Just as the Nashville passed the Farallon Islands outside San Francisco Bay, low clouds, high winds, and heavy seas became the norm, pitching and tossing the Nashville to an uncomfortable degree for the crew. After a week at sea the task force attempted to refuel from the Oiler Cimarron but heavy seas prevented it. The seas were so rough that two men were swept overboard from the Cimarron and one from the cruiser Vincennes, but all were rescued before hypothermia could set in. Finally, two days later the seas calmed and the Cimarron finally fueled the Nashville and the other ships. Task Force 18 then rendezvoused at dawn on April 13 and became part of Task Force 16 which consisted of flagship USS Enterprise (CV-6) under Admiral Halsey, heavy cruisers USS Salt Lake City (CA-25), USS Northampton (CA-26), USS Vincennes (CA-44) and escorting destroyers USS Balch (DD-363), USS Fanning (DD-385), USS Benham (DD-397), USS Ellet (DD-398), USS Gwin (DD-433), USS Meredith (DD-434), USS Grayson (DD-435), and USS Monssen (DD-436) along with supply ship USS Sabine (AO-25) and submarines USS Thresher (SS-200) and USS Trout (SS-202) north of Midway Island, itself a site for a future great naval battle that would turn the tide of the Japanese tsunami in the Pacific. The Battle of Midway itself was more than a little created and shaped by the task at hand. As soon as the ships were in formation Task Force 16 steamed west at high speed under a low cloud ceiling, perfect for hiding from enemy aircraft.

As if the nature and audacity of the mission of Task Force 16 was not risky enough, the Japanese in effect knew the Americans were coming. Unbeknownst to Admiral Halsey and the US government, Japanese naval radio intelligence had discerned the increase and nature of messages between Task Force 16, Task Force 18, and Pearl Harbor during the period of April 10-12, prior to the two forces joining. The Japanese knew the range of US Navy planes to be approximately 600 miles so they assumed the American carriers would have to close within at least 300 miles of Japan in order to launch any attack and be able to recover aircraft. It was a reasonable assumption, but the Americans were an unreasonable enemy. Sixty-nine bombers of the Japanese 26th Air Flotilla were on alert and flying up to 600 miles from the coast in order to locate and sink the American carriers and other ships prior to launching any attack against Tokyo. Additionally, the Japanese had scores of radio-equipped picket boats operating as an early warning system in a wide arc 600 miles out to sea. A betting man would place a bet accordingly on the Japanese.

The ships and submarines of Task Force 16 represented a sizeable portion of the operational combat ships of the US Navy in the Pacific at the time. In fact, it was almost half of the entire US Pacific Fleet. Hornet and Enterprise comprised half of the American carrier force in the Pacific Theater. Yet, compared to Japanese naval forces patrolling between them and their destination, they were in fact but a footnote. A footnote soon to make worldwide headlines and be directly responsible for tying up a large enemy fleet near Japanese home waters for much of the war and reinforcing the flawed Japanese strategy of forcing a massive showdown with the American fleet. The Nashville was one of the fastest ships in the US Navy. Her speed would be important during this mission as well as many others throughout her war service.

For the most part the voyage to the planned launch point 500 miles off the coast of Japan east of Tokyo was exactly as planned. It was ironic justice that for much of the trip Task Force 16 followed, in reverse, the same route that Japanese Task Force Kido Butai (Striking Force) did to launch the infamous attack on Pearl Harbor. And while the damaged inflicted would be considerably less, the psychological effect would be devastating and strategic in impact. It would literally traumatize the Japanese High Command and lead directly to the one of the most famous naval battles in history and a turning point in the Pacific naval war, the Battle of Midway.

The men of the Nashville went about their daily wartime routines during the voyage: eating, sleeping, standing watch, playing poker, tending to assigned work duties, and dealing with the maintenance needs of the ship which always seemed to include chipping off old paint and applying new coats. As Bud Varni said, "Sometimes I would hit the sack at night and the ship would be one color and when I awoke the next morning it would be a completely different camouflage scheme." He was not exaggerating. Nashville's battle dress for the mission was Measure Twelve Camouflage, a collection of navy blue, haze gray, and ocean gray designed to hide and alter the size, silhouette, and even perceived speed of the ship to Japanese surface and air forces.

On Friday, April 17, 1942 USS Nashville and the rest of Task Force 16 crossed the 180th Meridian and maneuvered for their final tanker refueling. During this refueling a little known incident occurred aboard Nashville that not only could have had a devastating and even fatal affect on the ship, but may have put the entire mission at risk of discovery by the Japanese. At about 0645 that morning Nashville came alongside tanker USS Sabine with the intent to take aboard 145,000 gallons of precious fuel. At 0738 a problem occurred when overflows were reported in the starboard fuel tanks and again at 0739. The starboard overflow tank itself started to fill creating a potentially dangerous situation if fueling was not shut down or the overflow problem rectified quickly. By 0739 and thirty seconds all firerooms reported that the tanks were

OK. But by 0740 and thirty seconds Lt. Gilliam reported to Lt. Brittan that oil was appearing at the port topside vent. Basis this and reports that tanks were being cut right and left, Lt. Brittan ordered all tanker fuel pumps stopped immediately. Clearly there was a dangerous problem that needed to be discovered and fixed. Seconds after this order it was reported that starboard and port tanks were still overflowing and the overflow tanks were dangerously filling at a rapid pace. Not more than thirty seconds later oil was coming out of both topside vents and the starboard oil tank was leaking into #1 and #4 firerooms. Nashville could have been taken out of the war with a single match. At this time an alert and brave crewman noticed a tank starting to actually bulge towards the fireroom and without hesitation he rushed to the filling valve and partially closed it, then moved forward just enough to tell crew topside to secure the pumps, then returned to the task at hand of completing the closing of the valve when the tank further bulged and burst at the top with tremendous and unfortunately deadly force. Oil was sprayed all over the #3 boiler and the starboard side of the fireroom and the danger of an instant fire and explosion did not deter for a moment the quick thinking and brave efforts of crewmen Coles, Bosier F1c, Royster CWT, Cowart WT1c, Weaver F1c, Irvine WT2c, and Bowman WT2c. As the engineering officer, Lt. Commander J. E. Fradd stated in his official report, "A fatal fire could and probably would have occurred except for the timely action of personnel on watch in #2 fireroom. These men are to be congratulated upon their excellent work in speedily and effectively handling this casualty." A simple spark would have triggered a devastating explosion, most likely destroying the Nashville and sending a massive fireball into the air that would have easily been noticed by the Japanese.

After the perilous refueling of the carriers and cruisers including Nashville, the task force proceeded west at high speed without the oilers and the submarine protection of the destroyers. The wind had increased to thirty-five knots and visibility was down to a dangerous one to two miles. As fate frequently plays the playwright, Radio station JOAK Tokyo was broadcasting that afternoon and at 1400 local time, "Tokyo Rose" explained to the Japanese public the logic of why Tokyo would never experience an enemy air attack. Nashville and the 10,000 sailors and eighty army aviators of Task Force 16 simply found that logic faulty.

The joke was on radio JOAK and the Japanese. Due to the zigzagging of the task force and strict radio silence, the Japanese miscalculated the arrival date of the Americans. That date had come and gone so the Japanese started to assume that perhaps the Americans had other target objectives.

Few if any battle plans are entirely executed as planned in the safety and sanity of an office and the Doolittle-Halsey plan to bomb Japan was no exception. But the sheer tenacity and inherent flexibility of the American command allowed it to be executed in a manner that generated the same spectacular results despite a critical logistical obstacle.

Radar was still relatively new and unrefined early in the war, often displaying information open to multiple interpretations, even among trained and skilled operators, but it did work and that gave an edge to the Americans. At 0310 on April 18 the radar operators on Enterprise noted something they did not expect nor want to see, the blips of what appeared to be two small ships approximately eleven miles distant, bearing 255 degrees. General quarters was sounded, awakening any crew sleeping as Admiral Halsey directed the task force hard to starboard at 350 degrees, successfully avoiding contact. Luck had been an ally, at least for the moment.

The morning of April 18, 1942 dawned with an overcast gray sky and heavy foreboding seas for Task Force 16. Intermittent rain squalls and thirty-foot swells sent waves crashing over the bow of Nashville with spray reaching the bridge, and even so the larger ships Hornet and Enterprise, with decks sixty feet above the waterline. At 5:58 AM one of the Enterprise's scout planes, patrolling forty miles out, spotted a Japanese patrol vessel. The scout plane immediately banked hard left and flew back to the Enterprise to warn the task force, still under strict orders to maintain radio silence in order to maintain the critical element of surprise. Pilot Lt. Osborne B. Wiseman hastily wrote that he had spotted an enemy patrol vessel at latitude thirty-six degrees, four minutes north, and longitude 153 degrees, ten minutes east, placed it into the canvas message bag, flew low and steady over the Enterprise, and his radioman tossed it onto the deck at 0715. Ominously, Lt. Wiseman also noted he thought he may have been sighted. Again the task force adjusted course and again luck apparently held. But it was a temporary hold.

At 0738 Hornet spotted yet another enemy patrol vessel barely and intermittently visible approximately ten miles distance. Japanese patrol vessel NO. 23, of the 5th Fleet, the Nitto Maru, was about to be introduced to the US Navy courtesy of the Nashville. There was no longer any doubt now that the Japanese knew the exact location of Task Force 16 and their destination. Luck had finally deserted the Navy.

The radioman on the Nitto Maru had sighted the task force and went below to advise his captain that two beautiful Imperial Navy carriers were in sight. The captain rushed on deck to see for himself and responded, "Yes, they are beautiful, but they are not ours." He promptly returned to his cabin below and shot himself in the head. The search was on for the Americans. Akagi Maru and Awata Maru immediately searched for the task force but could not locate the ships, and the same held for the Kisarazu Air Group of the 26th Air Flotilla.

Nashville had her own ears alert and picked up the trail also. Ron Neff, ARM2c who was not flying due to the impending launch of Doolittle's bombers said, "I was sitting down in the transmitter room fiddling around with the receivers and I got this code and it didn't make sense to me. I buzzed the Lieutenant up in the radio shack and he said to switch it over. It was that sampan out there." Later, after all the shooting was over, Ron received a call back from the Lieutenant. "He called me down later and said, 'I guess you heard the results of that,' and I did." Ron summed up the entire experience of the raid succinctly and accurately. "It was rather thrilling. A lot of it we did not understand until after it was done." Later, during his Nashville service Ron would down a Japanese Betty bomber and sink a Japanese submarine.

Admiral Halsey instructed the Nashville to sink the Japanese ship immediately. The Nitto Maru was 9,000 yards off the port bow of the Nashville. The seas were rough with fifteen-foot swells from the northwest. Nashville was already in Condition of Readiness II as general quarters sounded and the order to "commence firing" was given at 0750. Fire Control ordered Director I to train on target, still at approximately 9,000 yards. A ten-second salvo was ordered and commenced for spotting purposes. About this time Shipfitter William Smith heard someone in the aircraft hanger start singing, "Good-bye Mama, I'm off to Yokohama." Fire Control ordered "continuous fire" after spotting, but targeting was extremely difficult as the Nashville was rolling in the heavy seas and the Nitto Maru was either literally riding the crest of the waves like a fishing float or was totally obscured from view by those same waves. Joe Fales' battle station was in magazine Turret Five, "that's where the ammunition is in the canisters, and there was a strong aroma of the ether that preserves it. You'd pull the shell out of the shell casing, out of the canister." For a while, only Turret Two had the unobstructed firing opportunity and they were ordered by Chief Turret Captain Bob Zuck to "pour it on," and so they did.

A more difficult target that needed to be sunk quickly could not be imagined. At times it was impossible to see the target at all due to the swells, combined with the splashes of the six-inch projectiles. Nashville quickly swung to port to enable starboard firing on the target, reopening firing at a range of approximately 4,500 yards. Despite the difficulties presented by the rough seas, poor visibility, the size of the target, and the fact that some shells were believed to have passed completely through the vessel (only armor piercing shells were available at the time as opposed to high explosive bombardment shells which would have been more immediately effective against a thin-hulled vessel), Nashville sunk the Nitto Maru shortly after closing range with sinking occurring at 0823. "The sea was so rough it was only visible part of the time. We went into rapid fire and fired several hundred rounds before it sank. My battle station was shellman and I tried to remain calm as I loaded the 108 pound projectile. I weighed just thirty pounds more than it did," said Alan D. Ensor BM1c. It was believed that the Nitto Maru was equipped with a radio and both machine guns and a small cannon. Nashville reported two survivors in the water but circumstances prevented a rescue with at least one wounded survivor witnessed sinking beneath the surface by the commanding officer.

Nashville's work was not done despite the fact that by now it was generally believed the Nitto Maru got off a warning transmission received by Tokyo. Radiomen on the Nashville heard the Nitto Maru sent a message notifying Japan's Combined Fleet Headquarters that it had sighted three enemy carriers at its 0630 position 650 miles east of Inubo Saki, but sunk prior to answering Tokyo's request for clarification and further information. With the momentary lull in firing, the handling room petty officer called up the gun room and we asked what they had (been shooting at). He responded, "A battleship, a couple of cruisers, several destroyers, and a tanker. And then we started shooting again. Of course we didn't find out until later that they were feeding us a line," said Joe Fales. The second Japanese vessel engaged by Task Force 16 was sunk by Nashville at 1446. This vessel was first sighted by patrol planes from USS Enterprise and Nashville was instructed to sink her at 1409. Upon receiving orders Nashville quickly left formation and sighted the vessel at 1411, approximately 9,000 yards out. Since the Nitto Maru had already alerted Japanese headquarters of the presence of Task Force 16, Nashville held her fire and rapidly closed the range to a manageable firing distance. This vessel, unlike the Nitto Maru, was of wood construction, deemed slightly longer, and was painted black with the exception of a white deck house that was initially mistaken for a white flag of surrender. This proved unfortunate as Nashville was initially ordered to take prisoners first and then sink the ship. When this vessel then fired on Enterprise planes, the order was changed to sink her first and then recover any prisoners if time permitted. Nashville opened a deadly fire at 1424 and ceased firing at 1434 when it was seen that the vessel was sinking. When the Jap craft broke in two the 40MM anti-aircraft battery and the 20MM battery sank the forward half that contained the bridge.

Nashville then proceeded to pick up prisoners as ordered, stopping dead in the water and picking up five prisoners, numbers two through six of the war and the first ones taken since the crewman of the Japanese midget sub washed ashore in Hawaii on December 7, 1941 after the attack on Pearl Harbor. As Al Landi said, "All were shaken, bruised, and full of fuel oil." One of the prisoners was the sailor that first sighted what he thought were beautiful Japanese carriers and had in fact radioed the alarm to Tokyo. Marine CWO4 Raymond D. Chaney explained, "As they (Japanese) climbed up the ladder, our Chief Gunners Mate noticed that one of them had a knife in his teeth. The Chief aimed his pistol at him and said, 'Drop that knife or I'll blow your brains out!' The Jap evidently understood English because he dropped the knife. During interrogation later it was learned that he was a junior Jap naval officer." One prisoner was an American of Japanese descent who had returned to Japan prior to the war to visit relatives. Promptly drafted into the Japanese Navy, not an unusual occurrence, he swore to the Nashville interrogators he intentionally broadcasted incorrect information regarding the number of American ships sighted and their course, stating they were headed towards

Alaska. Harry C. Nadeau was one of several sailors and marines that escorted the prisoners to the brig. One injured survivor was immediately taken to Sick Bay. Al Landi was ordered to the foscle "to assist in pulling up the Jap survivors. I helped heave up two of them. One passed out at our feet when he reached the main deck. He was the one taken to Sick Bay and seemed to be the oldest of the patrol craft crew. He had a heavy black mustache." Albert L. Pender was also a direct witness to this historical capture of the Japanese.

During the first sinking action the Enterprise was recovering planes and the entire Task Force 16, with the exception of the Nashville, was making way at twenty-five knots away from Japan, literally leaving Nashville the closest American ship to Japan, the only American ship between Japan and the entire US Navy. No one on board had much time to recognize or consider what surely would have been an uncomfortable thought. And it was at this time that Tokyo Rose came to know the Nashville by name and later would erroneously call out her sinking several times throughout the war.

The radio report by Nitto Maru provided the Japanese with the first sighting of the US fleet in ten days, but when a confirmation was requested Nitto Maru had already been destroyed by Nashville. Yamato's Chief of Staff, Rear Admiral Matome Ugaki, promptly issued Order Number 3 (a plan never expected to be implemented, to repel an American fleet off the coast of Japan). By now Japan had mustered a massive force of 210 planes and two full naval task forces looking for the bold American attackers. Multiple carriers, cruisers, and destroyers were within a relatively short distance of the reported sighting including nine submarines. A formidable task force under Vice Admiral Chuichi Naguma that included the five fleet carriers *Akagi, Soryu, Hiryu, Zuikak,u* and *Shokaku* and heavy cruisers *Myoko, Haguro, Aito, Takao, Nachi,* and *Maya* was rapidly steaming back from the Indian Ocean and nearly at Taiwan. Calculating a launch point based on the range of carrier planes Ugaki reasonably expected the American task force to approach within 300 miles of the coast, so most forces, including the nine submarines were assigned to that area. But from the very beginning of the planning stages of this mission 'reasonable' was not a factor for the US Navy and their Army guests. It could be argued that not only the sighting of the Nitto Maru, but the understandable time involved for Nashville to sink her after she got off her first message but prior to sending a confirming message, may well have saved the entire task force. If the mission had gone to plan the Japanese would have been waiting at roughly the planned launch point and the task force would have had little chance to survive such an encounter. The fact that Nitto Maru did not send a second confirming message left just enough doubt in the minds of the Japanese that the B-25s were able to be launched and the task force was able to turn around and head back to Pearl Harbor, ducking into intermittent squalls all along the way to avoid detection. The Japanese Second, Fifth, and Sixth Fleets, and the 11th Air Fleet frantically raced to find the Americans but to no avail. At 1300 hours Tokyo time the Japanese Naval General Staff was informed that an enemy air raid was in progress over Tokyo.

Much has been made of Nashville's expenditure of 938 rounds of six-inch projectiles to sink the Nitto Maru, a small vessel of no more than seventy feet in length. But any such criticism was and is misguided and ill-informed at best. Halsey had instructed Nashville to sink the vessel as quickly as possible, the overriding factor being to attempt to prevent the vessel from radioing Japanese headquarters of the existence, location, and course of Task Force 16 lest the critical element of surprise be lost. Nashville was impelled to open fire immediately at a greater than ideal distance. The vessel was small in size and light in weight resulting in continuous and erratic movement with the large swells which kept the target literally obscured during much of the firing. Nashville herself was rolling due to the combination of swells and high speed in approaching the vessel (a characteristic of the long, sleek Brooklyn Class cruisers). The Nashville was loaded with armor-piercing shells resulting in multiple direct hits passing entirely through the vessel without explosive effect, which surely would have sunk it with one or two direct hits. Due to poor visibility there was not immediate evidence that the vessel had been hit and was rapidly sinking until it was obvious at which time Nashville ceased firing one minute later. And finally, "continuous fire" was initially engaged due to the desire to hit the vessel hard and quickly as opposed to the more common "rapid fire" or "salvo fire."

Nashville was at the forefront in the execution of "continuous fire," a term not familiar to even many in the Navy at the time and frequently confused with "rapid fire." "Continuous fire" in the case of the Nashville constituted a phenomenal rate of ten projectiles per minute per gun (one every six seconds) and Nashville had fifteen such six- inch guns. To view this in a mathematical sense, such a rate of fire was equivalent to the firing of one six-inch projectile every four-tenths of a second. Such an incredible rate would constitute up to 150 rounds per minute, an unbelievable rate for any ship at the time. In other words, the Nashville, when firing all fifteen six-inch heavy guns, put out a rate of fire equivalent to the 40MM Bofors anti-aircraft machine gun of the day which had a rate of 120-160 rounds per minute. It is easy for the most anal-retentive to understand how 900 plus rounds of shells could be used so quickly in the sinking of a small enemy vessel. Nashville took the self-proclaimed title of "Fastest Gunned Cruiser of WWII" and apparently kept that title until decommissioning.

While Nashville was taking on the outer defenses of the Empire of Japan the remainder of Task Force 16 was frantically but methodically going about the business of launching land-based US Army Air Force medium bombers from the short, wet, pitching wood deck of an aircraft carrier in rough seas while still 150 miles out from the planned launch point. Waves were crashing over the bow of the Hornet as Lt. Colonel Jimmy Doolittle and the crew prepared for takeoff. The bombers were so large that there was barely four feet of clearance between the starboard wingtip and the island superstructure of the carrier.

Doolittle's plane lumbered off the deck at 0824 just as the deck was pitching up, a necessary condition for the launch of each plane and a masterpiece of timing by the Navy Launch Officer. Following quickly behind was plane 2 piloted by Lt. Travis Hoover. Hoover would not only be saved by a Chinese man and fly seventy-one more missions in Europe in both B25s and P38s, he would bring that Chinese savior and his family to America after the war and eventually become neighbors and good friends with Nashville's Allan Ensor, completing a circle of circumstance and fate. By 0920 all planes had successfully launched and were Japan bound. "As a gun control officer of a battery of 20mm anti-aircraft guns I could see the planes take off," said Marine Raymond D. Chaney CWO. Samuel Sanders, at his battle station on Nashville for two straight days like the rest of the crew, saw the B-25s dip off the pitching deck of Hornet towards the sea and then finally angle up and away. Once the last plane safely took off Sanders and the rest of the Nashville crew let forth with a great cheer. "Everyone was so concerned about the pilots and crews," said Sanders. Already there were casualties as Hornet Machinist Mate Robert Wall was pushed by the high winds, pitching sea, and rain and prop backwash of plane 15, into the left propeller of plane 16, *Bat Out of Hell,* and lost his left arm. Men rushed to help him but *Bat Out of Hell* had to take off. As it did the plane's crew looked down at the still conscious sailor as he yelled, "Give them hell for me!" Later Wall's Hornet crewmembers would raise $1,800 for him. Combined with the weather and detection by the Nitto Maru and perhaps other Japanese vessels it was surely an ominous start to a mission inherently fraught with danger and poor odds. Going along with that was the fact that now, due to launching a day ahead of schedule as well as 150 miles further from their targets, the Chinese were not ready for them with their emergency airfields as planned. Ominous indeed.

Each of the bombers headed for their individually picked targets essentially on their own rather than in formation. And each of the crews knew they had an extra 150 miles to travel on limited gas already measured to the drop in gas cans that were to be manually poured into the tanks during the flight.

The Japanese had known for some time that the Americans were coming, but did not know when. They prepared by practicing with a mock air raid on Tokyo, with Japanese planes playing the role of the Americans. Doolittle's B25s so closely followed the Japanese drill that there was still surprise and little resistance, with no sirens heard by the public for almost twenty minutes after the planes were over the cities. The raid timing was impeccable.

Most of the planes attacked Tokyo but planes also hit Kobe, Nagoya, and Yokosuka as well. Of the sixteen bomber crews that took off from the pitching deck of the Hornet, four crash-landed, eleven bailed out, and one landed in Russia where Stalin immediately ordered them imprisoned from which they escaped some fourteen months later. Eight crewmen had the horribly bad luck of being captured by the surprised, humiliated, and angry Japanese. One man died of malnutrition, three men were executed (beheaded) against all international rules of war, and four tenaciously clung to life until they were rescued at the end of the war.

For morale and face-saving purposes Japanese radio, the very institution that touted the impossibility of US planes hitting the home islands, reported nine downed enemy bombers and the remainder fleeing in retreat. The Emperor had been promised the US fleet would be destroyed at Pearl Harbor and that was believed to be true, and barely four months later the heart of Japan, the capital city Tokyo was bombed and the life of the Emperor endangered. Losing face never had such need for more makeup.

American intelligence picked up a flurry of Japanese radio activity as would be expected. The powerful Nagumo task force and others was notified as they were just off the coast of Taiwan. Bomber strike forces were assembled in Yokosuka, aircraft were alerted on Wake Island for a possible search and strike on the returning Halsey task force. By the next day Japanese intelligence was reporting that the strike was from three American carriers and that the planes were in fact B-25s.

It was later reported by the Japanese that ninety buildings were destroyed (mostly factories, gas storage tanks, warehouses), fifty people were killed, and 250 injured. What they did not report was that the aircraft carrier Ryuho was damaged in dry-dock in Yokosuka. Unfortunately for Japanese civilians, military industrial plants coexisted alongside paper houses. Zoning was not a practice employed by the Japanese. Therefore, inevitably there were in fact civilian casualties of war.

In the Home Islands it was mass confusion and panic resulting from the first bombs falling. Office and government workers rushed to balconies and rooftops to see the spectacle for themselves, not quite believing what they saw, as the Americans once did during the initial stages of the Pearl Harbor attack. The Japanese had been told repeatedly by their government and military that American planes would never, ever fly over Japanese soil, and the people had the mindset that was true. What a shock the loud, fast, low-flying B-25s and their bombs must have been for the populace, including Hirohito. That mindset gave birth to one of the many rumors that immediately gained life that day, that their old enemies, the Russians, were launching a surprise attack of their own. The first government statements in broadcasts did not note the nationality of the planes and assured everyone that Hirohito was safe, the Imperial Palace in Tokyo untouched.

Military leaders experienced instant shame and loss of face, at least the Navy leaders did as the Army could not and would not be blamed for this impossibility. And it was the Navy that was responsible for and boasted of the safety from air attack of the Home Islands. Admiral

Yamamoto, the architect of Pearl Harbor, was said to be totally sullen and absolutely pale when advised of the attack. His failure to get the American carriers at Pearl Harbor, the very ones that just launched an inexplicable attack on the Home Islands, would now drive him ever more stubbornly towards a decisive battle policy, on the offensive, and would later result in the Battle of Midway.

Ironically, it was not the US but Japan via Radio JOAK Tokyo that announced the raid to an astonished world. But there were two separate broadcasts, one obviously not officially sanctioned. At 1345 a regular female announcer on JOAK stopped abruptly in her calm propaganda voice and let out an astonished scream followed by "A large fleet of enemy bombers appeared over Tokyo this afternoon causing much damage to military objectives and some damage to non-military objectives and some damage to factories. The known death toll is between 3,000 and 4,000 so far. No planes were reported shot down over Tokyo. Osaka was also bombed. Tokyo reports several large fires burning," and suddenly, her broadcast terminated. And then it was broadcast "Enemy bombers appeared over Tokyo for the first time in the current war. From their insignia they were seen to be American. Invading planes failed to cause any damage on military establishments." Both broadcasts were picked up by the Hornet and the first was relayed via semaphore to the rest of the task force. Cheers erupted on every ship. Still, the US government made no announcement, maintaining official silence while nervously waiting to hear any word of the raid's success, or equally likely, failure. Later, the first official statement was "American planes might have participated in an attack upon the Japanese capitol." This was an astonishingly noncommittal announcement perhaps reflecting the trepidation and up until then, bad news and lack of confidence experienced by the American military during the early stages of the war.

The newspapers were more direct. The *New York Times* reported "Japan Reports Tokyo, Yokohama Bombed By 'Enemy Planes' In Daylight" while the *New York Daily News* reported "U.S. Bombs Hit 4 Jap Cities." The *Columbus Evening Dispatch* was even more assertive, "US Warplanes Rain Bombs On Leading Cities Of Jap Empire; Yank Bombing Planes Carry War To Enemy; Tokyo, Yokohama, Kobe And Nagoya Hit In Three-Hour Offensive."

By April 21, 1942 Doolittle reported to the Army from an undisclosed location in China "Mission to bomb Tokyo has been accomplished." It was now safe to announce to the American public and the world the success of the daring raid. Yet, it was considered imperative to keep the true logistics of the raid top secret in order to keep Japan off balance and to protect any raids later in the war. James Hilton's novel *Lost Horizon,* set in a fantasy location in a Himalayan valley called *Shangri-La*, provided a creative and romantic solution for the president. During his April 21, 1942 press conference on the raid President Roosevelt was asked by a reporter the name of the base from which the bombers attacked Japan. Roosevelt answered, "They came from our new secret base at Shangri-La." The Japanese actually sent a force looking for this secret base which they thought was an island. It was with the passing of the first anniversary of the raid that the president finally told the American people of the Hornet's role in the raid and the execution of three flyers.

The Nashville crew and of Task Force 16 had every right to expect a grand celebratory homecoming upon arriving back at Pearl Harbor on April 25, but it was not to be. Like so much else regarding this historic and brave mission, it was kept secret. Admiral Halsey gave explicit orders that the mission was to be discussed with no one, not wives nor girlfriends, brothers nor sisters, nor parents nor friends. What would have gone down in history perhaps as the Halsey-Doolittle Raid did not as the Navy's part was not discussed, especially the role of the Hornet, for over a year, and by then the mission had taken on the moniker of "The Doolittle Raid." Japanese intelligence had noted the "coming of an enemy task force" into Hawaii on the twenty-fifth but they did not discern it was the Halsey-Doolittle task force. Everyone seemed equally in the dark.

Due to the secrecy of the mission there was no wartime citation given to Task Force 16 and as the years went by such acknowledgment seemed to be simply forgotten. However, after Bert Whited of Hornet's Scouting Eight brought it to the attention of Senator Robert C. Smith of New Hampshire, the injustice was rectified with a presentation at the Pentagon attended by over 100 Task Force 16 veterans on May 15, 1995 in a poignant ceremony. Task Force 16 was awarded the citation which read:

On the occasion of the 50th anniversary of the Second World War, it is appropriate that we take time to reflect on the unique and daring accomplishments achieved early in the war by Task Force 16. Sailing westward under sealed orders in April 1942, only four months after the devastating raid on Pearl Harbor , Task Force 16, carrying sixteen Army B-25 bombers, journeyed into history. Facing adverse weather and under constant threat of discovery before bombers could be launched to strike the Japanese homeland, the crews of the ships and LTC Doolittle's bombers persevered. On 18 April 1942 at 14:45, perseverance produced success as radio broadcasts from Japan confirmed the success of the raids. These raids were an enormous boost to the morale of the American people in those early and dark days of the war and a harbinger of the future for the Japanese High Command that had so foolishly awakened "The Sleeping Giant." These exploits, which so inspired the service men and women and the nation live on today and are remembered when the necessity of success against all odds is required.

(Signed) John H. Dalton
Secretary of the Navy
15 may 1995

The Task Force 16 Citation is awarded to the following ships, and all their personnel who participated in the Doolittle Raid:

- USS *Hornet* CV-8
- USS Enterprise CV-6
- USS Salt Lake City CA-25
- USS Northampton CA-26
- USS *Vincennes* CA-44
- USS *Nashville* CL-43
- USS *Balch* DD-363
- USS *Fanning* DD-385
- USS *Benham* DD-397
- USS *Ellet* DD-398
- USS *Gwin* DD-433
- USS *Meredith* DD-434
- USS *Grayson* DD-435
- USS *Monessen* DD-436
- USS *Sabine* AO-25
- USS *Cimaron* AO-22
- USS *Thresher* SS-200
- USS *Trout* SS-202

It is interesting to note that of these gallant ships only the Enterprise, Grayson, and Nashville survived the war.

"It is amazing that it took until '95 before it ever recognized that raid as being an important raid, when we all felt it was the turning point of the war and should have been recognized as such," said Joe Fales. "We all discussed it and we all felt that because of that raid they couldn't send as many aircraft carriers to Midway as they would have liked to. They could have sent all of their aircraft carriers and really pummeled us. But seeing as how we already hit them once, they were afraid to so they held some back." Such a point of view and argument are not without merit in the greater scheme of the war in the Pacific. Joe was quite correct in his assessment.

The war in the Pacific was still short of five months duration and already the Nashville and her crew had escorted convoys in the North Atlantic, transported the first American troops to Europe via Iceland and Marines to Wake Island, and participated in the first American offensive of the war with the first attack on the home islands of the Empire of Japan, the most famous naval raid in US history. But there was much more action to come and the newly battle-tested crew would soon be asked again to overcome superior enemy forces and be at the forefront of America's war with Japan.

"The Doolittle Raid, that was my first action, and believe me, it was a frightening thing for a twenty-year-old boy just off the farm. Well, we seen plenty more from then until December 13, 1944 when we caught a kamikaze that day," noted Norval Marion Jacks, Jr. SF1C.

Said Samuel Sanders, Seaman 1c "I was too young to be scared (seventeen). I was excited and wanted revenge for Pearl Harbor. It was very tough staying by your guns for so long after the attack. Everyone on the Nashville was a hero to me. The raid on Tokyo was a very dangerous act to perform; we were in great danger being so close to Japan."

Nashville firing at Nitto Maru during Doolittle Raid, April 18, 1942

CHAPTER 4
North to Alaska: Fog, Freeze, Bombs, and Boredom

***

"It was said that if one could see 100 feet ahead, it was a clear day."
-Allan Ensor

***

Upon returning to Pearl Harbor after the Doolittle Raid Nashville trained off Oahu for several weeks. Plans were afoot for Nashville to be a lone raider on another secret mission. Secret and perhaps suicidal. On May 4, 1942 Captain Craven sent a memorandum to all his officers that must have astounded as well as excited them to the possibilities inherent in yet another daring raid on the perpetrators of Pearl Harbor. The subject was planning for a raid on the Japanese fishing fleet operating east of Kamchatka with the intent to steam through the fleet at high speed, shooting at anything and everything, disrupting the vital food supplies of the enemy war machine. No matter that the very same fishing fleet was most likely to be guarded by more than a few heavy ships of the Imperial Japanese Navy.

The orders received by Captain Cravens read in part, "Patrol enemy fishing grounds and inflict maximum practicable damage to his fishing fleet, forces, and shipping." Nashville had free hand to do almost anything she wanted to do in terms of attacking the Japanese fishing fleet and of course, the Japanese navy that would no doubt be in attendance. Off limits were intentionally entering Russian territorial waters, damaging Russian ships, or wounding or killing their crews or hazarding the Nashville in any way to board ships or take prisoners (unlike during the Doolittle raid when Nashville stopped dead in the water to take on the survivors of the Nattu Maru).

The Nashville was fully expected to encounter various types of fishing vessels and the accompanying supply ships, cannery ships, and whale-oil processing ships, but also numerous Japanese naval vessels, specifically gun boats, torpedo boats, submarines, and light and even heavy cruisers along with land-based aircraft. Against this cornucopia of rich targets and multiple points of enemy firepower, Nashville was to sail alone and in secret. Additionally, it was considered that Nashville might well run into a Japanese task force intending to raid Dutch Harbor or other Alaskan points. While Nashville was expected to not engage such a force that could be expected to include destroyers, light and heavy cruisers, at least one battleship, and most likely a carrier, she was to "develop its character" and send out a warning report. "Develop its character" is Navy speak from officers in a safe rear area that translates to get close enough for Nashville's scout planes to sight the enemy force in a manner that would alert the Japanese of the presence of Nashville. More simply, let the overwhelmingly superior enemy force find you, like bait.

Captain Craven's preliminary plan was to "utilize the first day in a high speed dash, guided by air search, through the wide northern portion of the area, with the object of sinking as many of the supply ships and floating canneries as practicable, thereafter to mop up the smaller fishing vessels." Craven raised numerous insightful and important questions in his memorandum and asked officers to work on details of the plan in the areas of their own specialties and report to their department heads by noon on May 6, and then the department heads would prepare digests and discuss at a staff meeting on May 8.

Something else was happening on that day that ultimately affected the daring plans to raid Japan's food supply. Nashville had sailed to Midway, delivering Marines and supplies to the embattled island. Some crew had time to go ashore and see the damage done by the Japanese naval bombardment of a few weeks prior. Al Landi went swimming on the west beach, "the whitest and smoothest sand ever seen." At 0718 hours the Nashville was in the turning basin of Midway Lagoon, Midway Island, or so they thought when the ship ingloriously ran aground at the stern, damaging the rudder and the two after propellers. The steering efficiency of the ship was slightly impaired, particularly at low speed with rudder damage limited to the bottom. More seriously, the starboard after propeller lost a piece in one blade with the remaining blades bent and split while the port after propeller had all blades bent. Nashville was no longer capable of speeds above 18.7 knots without danger from excessive vibration. While there were a few explanations on how this could have occurred the final facts state the following: "the ship stern grounded approximately seventy feet north of the northerly boundary of the turning basin, the ship used a preliminary chart not approved that showed the area in question had been dredged but not yet dragged, the correct chart shows the area in question to have a depth of twenty-three feet (the ship had a stern depth of twenty-four feet, eleven inches), and the market buoy #3 was out of position." In any event, the incident sent the Nashville back to Pearl Harbor for repairs. Whether this had any effect on Nashville being assigned to flagship Task Force 8 in Alaska rather than continue duty as part of the fleet that would be involved in the battle of Midway is conjecture. On the surface it certainly appears so, but looking deeper there lies the secret orders to plan for a raid on the north Pacific fishing fleet by Nashville. In fact, Admiral Nimitz had plans for Nashville to conduct a radio simulation of a carrier task force off Midway, essentially to act as cheese in the trap set for Admiral Yamamoto's powerful task force headed towards the island. It is conjecture whether the Midway lagoon mishap saved Nashville from destruction but it most certainly did keep her from carrying out a brave task of naval deception and the timing probably kept Nashville from at least starting her dashing run through the Japanese fishing fleet with guns ablaze.

On May 14, 1942 she departed the warm waters of Hawaii, trailed by a school of leaping dolphins for miles, and steamed towards Kamchatka at ten knots during the night and seventeen knots during the day, to carry out her orders to raid the Japanese fishing fleet. Well before arriving near Kamchatka she received new orders to proceed to Dutch Harbor, Alaska at course 040 and twenty-two knots to become flagship of Read Admiral Robert A. Theobold's Task Force 8, known as the North Pacific Force, leading eight other ships with orders to defend Alaska including the far flung and desolate Aleutian Islands. She maintained zigzagging and aerial anti-submarine patrol throughout the voyage. Japan, despite the stunning success of the Doolittle Raid, remained undefeated with her Navy and had not yet suffered a capital ship loss in the war. Driven by arrogant confidence fed by a sense of national superiority, a militaristic culture and a phenomenal string of victories, General Hideki Tojo, the Japanese Premier, pointed the Nippon dagger of expansion towards Midway and the Aleutian Islands, American continental territory.

American intelligence in the form of Admiral Nimitz's overworked code breakers had discerned that the Imperial Combined Fleet would depart Japanese waters approximately May 20 and sea and air attacks against Midway Island (a part of the Hawaiian Islands) and the Aleutian Islands would occur sometime around May 24. Nimitz had but two carriers assuredly available, Enterprise and Hornet, and a small number of cruisers, including Nashville, and destroyers available to meet an anticipated Japanese attack fleet that included six aircraft carriers and eleven battleships and scores of other ships. The Joint Chiefs of Staff debated whether to concentrate all available ships at Midway or to split off a task force to defend the Aleutians. Ultimately it was decided that the United States could not allow the Japanese to invade the Aleutians and possibly take Dutch Harbor, leaving Alaska open for occupation and cut off the sea lanes to Siberia. Consequently, Nashville was chosen as the flagship of Task Force 8 and ordered to the Aleutians. Her duty would not be without combat.

Aboard Nashville Admiral Theobald received orders that stated he was to "oppose the advance of the enemy in the Aleutian-Alaskan area, taking advantage of every favorable opportunity to inflict strong attrition," and "be governed by the principle of calculated risk." Did this mean sacrifice the nine ships of Task Force 8 if that means stopping the Japanese from landing on American territory and provide them a launching point against the Seattle? Yes, it did. More worrisome was information from CINCPAC dated May 25 that stated two Japanese aircraft carriers were a probable part of the Japanese attack force along with three seaplane tenders, three heavy cruisers, two light cruisers, twelve destroyers, eight submarines, an undetermined number of seaplane type heavy bombers, troop transports, and cargo vessels. Woefully unprepared, the Navy presence in Alaska on December 7, 1941 consisted of less than 600 men, seventeen minutes estimated ammunition supply, and nothing bigger than several PBY scout planes. Once again, Nashville was part of an outgunned and outmanned task force facing overwhelming odds. And the question remained: exactly where would the Nashville and her task force ships fight the Japanese? The Aleutian Islands had yet to be mapped in any meaningful detail. No matter, the job had to be done. If the Japanese took Alaska they would be only three hours bombing distance from Seattle, home of Boeing and the Bremerton Navy Yard. Alaska was closer to Tokyo than to New York. Alaska, including the Aleutians, had to be a last line of defense for Canada and the US mainland.

Nashville steamed into the icy waters of Dutch Harbor on May 26 in a big hurry to leave. But it took several hours just to dock her since the facilities were not set up for a ship so large. Once docked, she stayed just long enough to drop off and load supplies, then departed to Kodiak May 28, 1942. After embarking Admiral Theobald at 1310 from USS Reid, she sailed from Women's Bay, Kodiak June 2 with USS Sabine and USS Humphreys to rendezvous with the remainder of hastily assembled Task Force 8 coming in from multiple points across the Pacific. By the time all ships assembled on June 3 in bitter cold, blinding wind, and violently pitching seas to establish a defensive picket line, the Japanese had already passed the area undetected. Dutch Harbor radar picked up incoming bogies at 0540 and moments later a young yeoman frantically tapped out an un-coded message: "About to be bombed by enemy planes." Such dangerous lack of protocol and stealth infuriated Admiral Theobald and his staff aboard Nashville. Lack of protocol notwithstanding, the yeoman was completely accurate. Shortly thereafter, Flight Leader Lieutenant Masauki Yamaguchi's attack force from carrier Ryujo struck Dutch Harbor, sinking a permanently docked old Steamer they thought to be the Nashville. At nearly the same time the Battle of Midway was about to commence.

Under strict radio silence and a wave-hugging thick blanket of fog, Task Force 8 searched for the Japanese Fleet under Admiral Kakuta, in a sweep 500 miles from Dutch Harbor. Neither the ships nor land-based air patrols and bombers were able to see and make contact with the Japanese. They often could do neither for their own fleet in the fog. On June 4 the Japanese struck yet again at 0107 hours with the Fourth Carrier Division and part of the Fourth Cruiser Division and then quickly retired south under orders from Admiral Yamamoto after the stunning American victory at Midway. But the Japanese left something behind in their withdrawal; army landing forces took the Aleutian islands of Attu and Kiska, occupying American territorial soil. While eluding Nashville's Task Force 8 with a major assist from the weather, Admiral Boshiro Hosogaya's Northern Force had won the latest campaign of the Battle of Alaska, he had set up strong land and air bases on Attu and Kiska islands (five times zones from Juneau), effectively taking westernmost Alaska. Now Nashville and others had to fight the Japanese in American territorial waters and American soil.

By the evening of the 4th the Battle of Dutch Harbor may have looked like a standoff but still the Japanese Fleet was yet to be located by Task Force 8. Admiral Theobald had received constant reports during the day but the ordered radio silence restricted his communication to line of site blinker signals, of dubious value in the fluid artic weather conditions. But when he was informed of the second attack on Dutch Harbor he was not about to wait for a third so he ordered the Nashville to leave behind the task force and make a top speed run, alone and without escort, through the rough seas to Kodiak. Nashville sped into Kodiak early on June 5 where she received a PBY report of a Japanese task force in the Bering Sea with two carriers making high speed directly for Dutch Harbor. Nashville operating alone against large Japanese naval forces was becoming an uncomfortable and dangerous habit.

Due to artic weather, lack of equipment, and poor communications, both elected and imposed by extenuating circumstances, confusion was not uncommon. On June 10, Army Captain Robert E. "Pappy" Speer, flying a LB-30 Liberator, flew down through a clearing in the fog over Kiska to scout the harbor. Ships were sighted and thought to be the Nashville and her task force, but due to radio silence proper identification could not be made via voice, so the Liberator dove low over the ships and was greeted with a barrage of anti-aircraft fire. Captain Speer and his co-pilot Frederick Ramputi were furious as they believed they had been fired on by the Nashville. Back at base at Unmak a Navy officer explained that they had been fired on not by the Nashville but by a three-stack Natori-class cruiser. At least part of the Japanese fleet had been momentarily located, if not by textbook means.

After much heated discussion in Washington, DC on strategy and the question of letting the Japanese have Kiska, containing them or driving them off the island, orders came from Roosevelt to San Francisco to Pearl Harbor to Alaska: "Fight back. Push the enemy into the sea. Get Kiska back." And so the long and arduous process began for one of the most forgotten, environmentally hostile and remote offensive campaigns of the entire war.

Aboard Nashville Admiral Theobald ordered all available planes, including Nashville's own scouts, to search the area of the Bering Sea and Nashville dutifully steamed into the unknown on the same search for the elusive Japanese carrier fleet. Nothing of note occurred except the "Battle of the Pribilofs" in which six new, straight from the Boeing plant in Seattle, B-17 Flying Fortresses with nervous green crews and new radar dropped tons of bombs on a radar target of what was believed to be Japanese ships. They almost sunk the miniscule Probilof Islands. But the game of searching for the larger, more powerful enemy would continue for five more days for the Nashville and her fellow ships until it was determined that the PBY report was in error. Admiral Theobald then transferred his flag ashore at Kodiak after the Nashville docked.

Just as Nashville and her fellow cruisers and destroyers were searching for the Japanese Northern Fleet, so too were the Japanese searching for the Nashville task force, albeit with a much larger force. Nashville continued its unenviable habit of being matched up against far superior Japanese forces. Admiral Yamamoto assumed the Americans would counter-attack in Attu and Kiska so he sent two more carriers, Zuiho and Zuikaku, and their escorts to join Admiral Kakuji Kakuta's already formidable fleet of carriers Ryujo and Junyo and numerous cruisers and destroyers. Nashville and a few determined friends were now facing literally the largest and most powerful navy force anywhere in the entire Pacific Ocean. Admiral Spurance's Task Force 16 with carriers Enterprise and Hornet, flush with their stunning victory at Midway, would steam north towards the Aleutians but they were only halfway there by June 10. But American forces were light in the Central and South Pacific so Admiral Nimitz regretfully recalled Task Force 16. Nashville and others remained the only force in the Aleutians to stand against the Japanese. Orders from Nimitz to Admiral Theobald aboard Nashville were to keep a high degree of pressure against the Japanese, continue to seek them out and harass them, be on the offensive, and keep the Japanese on the defensive. And so they did.

Nashville and the ships of Task Force 8 continued patrolling for another two months in conditions of extreme cold, heavy seas, wind and rain, snow and fog. It had that rare combination of simultaneous gale force winds and thick fog, an ungodly duo for a sailor. Allan Ensor BM1c said, "It was said that if one could see 100 feet ahead, it was a clear day." Albert L. Pender MM1c thought "it was the foggiest place I can ever remember." Nashville did lose a scout plane and pilot to the weather but later learned that the pilot was rescued and assigned to another cruiser. Clear days per year for most Aleutian Islands could be counted on both hands, with a finger or two left over. Only the tropical Japan Current from the south kept the oceans from freezing over each winter.

The fog and cold had other unanticipated consequences. Albert U. Gaines had mess duty for a long portion of the ship's Alaskan duty and one of his jobs was cutting the butter and placing it on trays due to the cold weather. "When butter does not spread easily or at all, men consume more of it by default." Albert noted the results: "We used a lot of butter on our toast and gained weight while in the Aleutians." Delbert Ford SF2c volunteered to do the standing lookout watch at night on the outboard side of the .25 caliber guns, "I volunteered to stand this watch because they would play big band music over the sound power phones. I liked it better than standing in a deck gear locker in the dark." And if the music was not playing, the big band tunes of GM3c George Bustin's wailing harmonica washed over the ship from the aft Gun Director position. Other duty was less desirable, like that of Harold G. O'Hara MM1c who had to constantly work hard to keep the whaleboats free of ice (a near impossibility) and operable. Others had to deal with the mundane task of loading supplies from supply ships and at times loading them in warehouses ashore, always in very cold weather it seemed. Joe Fales and men from other ships worked all night unloading groceries from the supply ship bridge and stacking them in the assigned corner of the warehouse. The only problem was that with all the activity going on no one came in to feed them or relieve them for the mess hall. So after working until approximately 0500 hours Joe, despite the prevalent signage that warned of a general court martial for eating any of the food, was so famished that he broke into a gallon can of peaches and a tin of soda crackers. Sure enough, the storekeeper came in and caught them all eating. "He marched us right down and into the office," remembers Joe. "That Lieutenant was going to have our hide until I told him how long it'd been since we'd been fed. Then the storekeeper got chewed out and they took us straight down to the mess hall and fed us. And nothing more was said about it."

Attempts to bombard Japanese positions on Kiska on July 22 and July 27 were cancelled due to the fact that the island itself simply could not be seen at all through the heavy, snowy fog. Each time Nashville had to withdraw for the night. Nashville's group of fourteen ships, including heavy cruiser Indianapolis (now flagship of Admiral Theobald), light cruisers St. Louis, Honolulu, and Louisville, along with nine destroyers continued to brave the zero visibility fog, attempting to get close to the island yet barely avoid running aground on the dangerous reefs. There were inevitable accidents in these dangerous conditions. Two destroyers collided and then another rammed a fourth destroyer. Four of fourteen ships were now out of commission and the task force had yet to see the island and fire a shot. With escalating frustration they retired back to Kodiak. At Kodiak Nashville benefited from a USO show and was visited by Edgar Bergen and his two cohorts, Charlie McCarthy and Mortimer Snerd, and given a two hour show in the hanger on the hanger deck. But that was not all of the fun some of the crew experienced in Kodiak. Sailors, of any age being sailors, and Kodiak being a frozen Wild West town, it was a given that some of the men partied until they dropped, literally. Patrick Carigan FC3c was there. "They would send dump trucks into town to pick the ones that could not walk. Many passed-out sailors were hauled back to the dock in dump trucks and laid out on the dock. They would announce on the ship, 'would one Petty Officer from each division report to the dock to identify the liberty party.' A Petty Officer from each division was required to identify people from his division before they were brought aboard Nashville. Luckily I was able to survive liberty without being carried onto the ship." Many others were understandably not in the frigid, remote conditions.

Others did more unusual things on their liberty jaunts, men such as Bev Bevington of N Division who went, along with others, bear hunting. Some men fished from the side of the ship, easily pulling large salmon from the icy waters. Both Kodiak and Kiska looked like an old west town straight from a John Ford western, down to the wooden sidewalks, incessant mud, weathered wooden storefronts, and even a few wooden Indians. Men rode into town on buses and came back to the docks on the same if they were still capable of walking. But before they arrived back at the dock, each bus had to pass a checkpoint where SPs checked each man for booze, which of course was illegal to bring aboard ship. Joe Fales remembers how some men "would buy hot water bottles, fill full (with alcohol) and strap it around their waist or in the crotch. At times somebody would try to put a pint or something on the ankle and if the

Marines found out about it they would hit it with the nightstick and bust the bottle." And probably the poor sailor's heart.

And there were yet more ways sailors spent liberty time amusing themselves but still, alcohol seemed to almost always be involved. Joe Fales and friends decided to have an old fashioned, simple picnic at the lake above the bay. They dutifully packed sandwiches and apples and not surprisingly, beer. While hiking towards the lake they happened upon a small creek populated with stunning abundance of salmon and trout, a fisherman's dream. But they did not need fishing gear to fish in this virgin stream. "The creek was only five, maybe ten feet wide and you could stand in the water, which was icy cold of course, and reach down and the fish would swim between your legs. You could grab them and throw them up on the shore." And they did so until they had a very large indeterminate number of fish flopping around on the ground. But while they were fishing in this manner they were also drinking beer, apparently as fast as they were picking up fish. Gradually the beer had more force upon body and mind than a hefty salmon haul and the fish were soon forgotten. Philosophically, Joe Fales said, "I suppose some bear had a real good meal there." The fish fry never happened that day.

There occurred a commonly known but little discussed incident aboard Nashville during those long, frigid, and frustrating months in the Aleutians. Reportedly, during one of the bombardments, two sailors were discovered *flagrante delicto* in a storeroom area. "Imagine that," as Eddie "Moscow" Yusko exclaimed, "two guys doing it in the middle of a battle." Indeed, it was a shocking and serious offense, not only of a dereliction of duty but also of all military rules, navy notwithstanding. All whispered comments and jokes regarding men being at sea for months and stories of old 'pirates' aside, homosexuality or homosexual acts, while no doubt a fact of life in WWII as in any other time, were not tolerated in the slightest if reported up the chain of command and were generally dealt with in Draconian style.

One of the sailors involved, a young man from San Francisco of all places, was brought before the Captain on suitable charges. Reportedly, when the Captain inquired if he had anything to say for himself he replied, "Captain, you do it your way and I do it my way." That of course was more than an admission of guilt and in no way helped his situation. Apparently, this sailor had names of like-minded men in a small notebook and a ship- wide investigation was undertaken. As it turned out, he had listed names of a handful of sailors and marines in order to falsely implicate them, probably a payback for a slight or offense of some sort. At the conclusion of the investigation, a number of men, thought to be as many as a dozen total, were arrested and ingloriously removed from the ship in leg irons. No matter how miserable duty in Alaska was, it was infinitely preferable to the much longer term fate that awaited these men. It was common for such men to be sentenced to eighty-five years in military prison, a life sentence if fully served.

News of the incident, investigation, and removals spread faster than war rumors. It caused embarrassment and more for the crew. On a bus taking men from several ships into town for liberty, a remark was made to the effect that Nashville was a "queer" ship and fights erupted, causing the bus driver to pull over and Shore Patrol to be summoned. Several times, with Nashville tied up alongside but not dockside to the Indianapolis, meaning the crew had to walk across the deck of the Indianapolis to reach the dock, similar remarks were made and again, fights were the result. Eventually it all ended but it was a source of irritation for a short time. Meanwhile, the war continued unabated.

Admiral Theobald was ordered to stay in his office for reports and communications with superiors so he ordered Real Admiral William W. "Poco" Smith to take command of the remaining ten ships and return to Kiska for another attempt at bombarding the Japanese on Kiska. They tried still again on August 3, probing through the fog but to no avail. Undaunted, Nashville and the rest of the task force tried again late on August 7. The minesweepers went ahead for sweeping operations, followed by the destroyers as Nashville led the cruisers Honolulu and St. Louis followed by heavy cruisers Indianapolis and Louisville. The Indianapolis of course was to become famous later in the war, for all the wrong reasons. At 1630 Nashville and the rest of the task force entered a zero visibility fog bank at twenty knots, literally not able to see a couple of yards from the ship and then, ninety minutes later the fog abruptly and completely cleared. Nashville and another cruiser quickly launched two scout planes each but then almost immediately the fog descended, currents shifted, and it was impossible for the task force to determine where they were much less where Kiska might be located. The St. Louis was directly astern of Nashville and suddenly materialized in the fog and came rushing towards the ship's stern. Joe Fales was on the stern. "I was standing there looking up at it. Now I want you to know, the bow of that Brooklyn Class cruiser coming out of the fog looked like the iceberg must have looked to the Titanic, because it was huge." The St. Louis immediately backed off and got back into position. They tried yet again at 1934 hours and soon shouts of "Land Ho!" as if in the days of sail, were emanating from the leading destroyers. The fog lifted to 300 feet off the sea and there sat, practically in the laps of the crews, the snow-capped jagged and barren mountains of Japanese-occupied Kiska. "It was pea-soup thick and suddenly the fog lifted momentarily and we could clearly see Kiska and the Japanese and all hell broke loose as we immediately opened fire," said GM3c George L. Bustin, and it was his friend, Patrick Carigan FC3c who was in Plot III and had his finger on the trigger of those guns. "We could see smoke from the tank explosions and we could hear the Jap planes overhead in the fog," said Marine Raymond D. Chaney CWO.

Finally, the Navy had its first Alaskan campaign counterattack as Task Force 8 bombarded Japanese shore installations, troop concentrations, landing craft, several bombers, and a cargo ship. The Japanese returned fire from shore batteries but made no hits on the ships. After months of frustration and thousand of miles searching in the harshest weather conditions, the crews were ready and eager. Fire was so rapid that ammunition for most of the task force was depleted within seven minutes. Nashville fired 1096 rounds of ammunition. And yet damage done was minimal for such a bombardment as firing was done blind, firing over a ridge at targets not quite seen and not well marked by the Army air force as their scout planes, along with several of those from the task force, were harassed by superior forces on the island. For the most part Japanese installations on the 4,000 foot volcanic coned and twenty-two-mile-long island were on the northern and western downslopes and could not be seen by ships nor planes. It was a valiant effort but frustrating, a common combination for fighting in the Aleutians. But damage was done. And Nashville's five-inch battery was credited with downing one Japanese Zero and one of the destroyers, yet another. Captain Taisuke Ito had just arrived for inspection of the island's defenses and quickly jumped into a foxhole as the first shells fell. He watched the naval shells "fall like rain" on the installations. Beached landing barges were obliterated, a barracks blew up and burnt to the ground, three seaplanes were destroyed, and a freighter severely damaged (and sunk the next day courtesy Army PBYs). On board Nashville Marine Raymond D. Chaney "could hear the Jap Zero fighter planes in the fog above but of course they could not see to attack us." It was the first and last bombardment of Kiska in 1942.

But the situation was to get worse. The Navy had been hit hard at Savo Island where it and the Australians had lost four cruisers and two destroyers and the Marines were holding precariously to a miniscule beachhead on Guadalcanal. More ships were transferred from the North Pacific Force defending Alaska, leaving the entire Alaskan theater with only four old destroyers, several smaller support ships, and two light cruisers, including the Nashville. As it had been since the war started, Nashville faced daunting odds against a larger and more powerful enemy. Many in the crew thought that at some point, those odds would catch up with them.

On August 28 Nashville departed Kodiak to escort an Army landing force to establish a forward base at nearly uninhabitable Adak Island, midway in the Aleutian chain. It was the same incessant fog and wind and cold both to and from Adak but without any sight of the Japanese fleet. On August 30 beloved, revered Captain Craven was transferred as Nashville's commanding officer and Captain Adolphus Spanagel USN took the helm.

The continuing liberties in Alaska were no more refined than the weather and accommodations. Rich Egles had shore patrol duty. "There were lots of saloons with a Wild West atmosphere. One saloon had a huge Kodiak bear trophy. It was a favorite among the sailors. Fights between crews were fairly common but quickly controlled by Navy Shore Patrol. I had shore patrol duty in the Red Light District. No one was allowed in the 'House' showing any signs of inebriation. They had to be very mannerly and respectful. The visits were allowed and controlled by the Navy." While sweethearts back home may have been surprised and aghast as such a situation had they known, and they did not, it was a fact of life in a lonely, desolate war zone for thousands of young men.

During September and October Nashville continued her patrol operations in the Aleutians and Northern Pacific, constantly fighting 100 plus knot winds and icy seas of up to seventy feet crashing over the bow, all the while looking for Japanese ships and submarines. Once the starboard screw guard was damaged when the Nashville was refueling a destroyer and the heaving seas sent it crashing down on that extended part of the ship, sending a shiver of vibration throughout the ship and making many wonder if they had hit a mine that did not explode or even a Japanese submarine. It was tough, miserable duty. Joe Fales said, "When I stood watches on the bridge as helmsman, I just wrapped my arms around the wheel. There was no way you could hold a course like I had always held it before. The crests of the waves were breaking over the bridge and that was four decks above the main deck, four stories high. It wasn't a pleasant experience." Crashing waves could quickly freeze and endanger the ship with excessive and uneven weight so the crew was to chip off the ice as it formed. An unimaginably uncomfortable experience.

It wasn't any better during the storms to be below decks. Normally men who had bunks to sleep in were considered lucky as opposed to those that had to sleep in the timeless and back-breaking sailor's hammock. But in the stormy seas of the Aleutians, those in the bunks had to strap themselves in lest they literally be tossed out of their bunks, hurtling across the decks and into bulkheads, while the hammock men swayed at times almost violently, or more accurately stayed constant with gravity and up and down while the ship swayed around them. Huge urns of hot coffee were suspended and swaying at all times but readily available to any that braved the internal elements for a cup of joe. The mess hall was always wet and the coffee hot and the ship rolling and pitching, so the potential for accidents was always real.

Patrols not only involved looking for the Japanese fleet to one degree or another, it meant interdicting commercial shipping traffic in and around the ports. This involved at times, members of the Nashville crew boarding ships in search of contraband and even Japanese military personnel (the US was not always so sure how Japanese soldiers made it to islands like Attu when no Japanese fleet had been tracked). Ed 'Moscow' Yusko, one of seven brothers in the service, had such duty frequently. "I spoke Russian so I interpreted while we were in the Aleutians. We thought the Russians were smuggling in Japanese so we boarded their ships and some of them were like pigpens. They had women, kids, cows, pigs, chickens, they lived like that. But we had a hunch they were smuggling in Japs and they were, they were all over the place up in Dutch Harbor."

The popular and respected Captain Craven

Edward "Moscow" Yusko

Nashville's "eyes" above, the scout plane

Nashville firing on Japanese position ashore, Alaska

CHAPTER 5
War in the Pacific: Tragedy Strikes

***

"There were many acts of bravery, too numerous to mention."
-Leon A. Higginson

***

It was no small sense of joy for the crew when orders were issued for the Nashville to proceed south from Dutch Harbor to Hawaii and liberty in sunny and warm Honolulu with its white beaches, tropical breezes, and real bars. Excepting orders for home leave, it was the best order the crew had ever received. Nashville arrived at Pearl Harbor on November 22. War or not there were always routines to follow and inspections to endure. Allan D. Ensor BM1c, like everyone else, had to deal with them all. "During a personal inspection on deck," remembers Allan, "a seagull did its number on me that caused a muffled laughter in the ranks. When our division officer, Lt. John Carmichael, saw what happened he said, 'Ensor, you have my permission to swear, but do so when you go below to change your jumper.'" Essentially all of the crew received and took all liberty possible on Oahu, thawing out from their Alaskan tour on the beach at Wikiki, visiting the Sheraton or Royal Hawaiian for drinks and the aforementioned houses of pleasure, sightseeing, sleeping, watching movies, and dating the locals. The ship departed Pearl Harbor on December 17 and sailed into the Southwest Pacific in the company of destroyer USS Ralph Talbot and Army transport Frederick Funston. In days she arrived at Nandi, Fiji Islands and prepared to add her firepower to the ongoing battles for control of the hotly contested Solomon Islands, including Guadalcanal.

The voyage from the artic Aleutians to the steamy Solomons meant that Nashville crossed over the International Date Line, an imaginary north-south line that marks the end of one day and the beginning of another on the calendar, responsible for the strange phenomenon of experiencing two Christmas days (which the Nashville did once) or skipping a day altogether. Sailors are a superstitious and tradition-bound lot. The crossing, something Nashville did fourteen times during her tours of duty, was cause for ritual, horseplay, a touch of good-intentioned cruelty, and good fun. It was also a time of initiation into a select secret society of mariners. No one, neither officers nor dignitaries nor heavy weight boxing champions, was exempt from the rituals, including the visiting former boxing champ Gene Tunney. The ritual of crossing the date line differed slightly from one time to the next, from ship to ship, from navy to navy, and from one period of history to another. But what remained constant was tradition and sense of moving into an accomplished society, of moving from being a "polliwog" to a "shellback" and, of course, the playful and at times humiliating process shellbacks put polliwogs through. Men were at times blindfolded and paraded through lines of waiting sailors that alternately dumped garbage (fruit rinds and cold oatmeal were favorites) on them, covered with engine grease, tossed into a makeshift pool on deck that the vulnerable blindfolded polliwog thought was the ocean, attacked with high pressure water hoses, dressed in costumes ranging from baby diapers made of sheets to something resembling a bathrobe and slippers, painfully poked at with electrically charged flatware, had their heads shaved and chest hair removed, sometimes by cutting, other times by shaving, dumped into a garbage pit, and just generally scared, beat, laughed at, and humiliated. It was not all that unlike an initiation into a college fraternity, only probably much scarier, painful, and far more elite. Charles R. Conrad remembers "crossing the equator and seeing a Navy Lieutenant JG standing on the bow wearing only his skivvies and looking for Davey Jones through the bottom of a set of Coca-Cola bottles." No man escaped the initiation, nor would they want to. Polliwogs that transformed into shellbacks received a colorful and official proclamation document stating:

> "To all sailors wherever ye may be: and to all Mermaids, Whales, Sea Serpents, Porpoises, Sharks, Dolphins, Eels, Skates, Suckers, Crabs, Lobsters and all other Living Things of the Sea. Greeting: Know ye that on this X day of X, 194X, in Latitude 00000 and Longitude (Censored) there appeared within Our Royal Domain the USS Nashville bound south for the Equator and for Operation At Sea. Be

It Remembered, that the said Vessel and Officers and Crew thereof have been inspected and passed on by Ourself and Our Royal Staff. And Be It Known: By all ye Sailors, Marines, Land Lubbers and others who may be honored by his presence that (name of crewman) having been found to be worthy to be numbered as one of our Trusty Shellbacks he has been duly initiated into the Solemn Mysteries Of The Ancient Order Of The Deep. Be It Further Understood: That by virtue of the power invested in me I do herby command all my subjects to show due honor and respect to him wherever he may be. Disobey this order under penalty of Our Royal Displeasure. Given under our hand and seal this (date). Davey Jones, His Majestys' Scribe. Neptune Rex, Ruler of the Raging Main. By His Servant (captains name)".

Christmas Day 1942 was spent anchored off the idyllic island of Fiji. Swimming in the warm clear water was allowed that afternoon off port side. But it was not swimming like you remember as a kid. A torpedo/anti-submarine net enclosed the swimming area and several sailors were stationed upon the superstructure with machine guns, all as a protection against a possible shark attack. Never mind that machine gunning swarming sharks may well dump so much blood into the water as to attract even more in a feeding frenzy. But such an action was not needed and men like Joe Fales and George Bustin enjoyed their Christmas swims immensely.

***

Heavyweight champ Gene Tunney during the sacred Neptune transformation of "polliwog" to "shellback"

MUNDA (January 43)

While the Japanese were taking a beating from the Marines on Guadalcanal, receiving a trickle of fresh troops only via submarine, they were attempting reinforcing and building up of their strength in the Central Solomons and New Guinea. Northwest of Guadalcanal, on New Georgia Island, the Japanese decided to build an airstrip. And they did so for good reason. This location would allow them to hit Henderson Field on Guadalcanal, only 175 miles southeast, allowing strafing and bombing with larger loads and much more time over the target. On November 24, 1942 a Japanese task force laid anchor at Munda Point on New Georgia Island and soon thereafter work started on the "Munda Emergency Airfield."

Showing a learning curve in operations and tactics not often exhibited during the war, the Japanese used ingenuity in the building of the airfield in attempting to keep its existence and work unknown to the Americans. Navy and Marine pilots had not been able to see anything new at Munda other than a few small buildings. But on December 3 a photoreconnaissance mission showed something odd under the canopy of trees. Subsequent mission photographs studied in detail discerned that the Japanese were in fact building an airfield under the palm fronds of the coconut trees. As a tree needed to be removed for construction, with the help of a tree-top height guidewire grid laid out along the lines of the coconut plantation, replacement palm fronds were attached to the guidewires, resting above the field itself. Close analysis of the photos revealed a large airstrip of 2,000 feet and anti-aircraft gun emplacements. P-39s Airacobras out of Henderson Field attacked the airstrip but it did little more than slow the construction process as repairs were made immediately and construction continued.

After completion the Munda Airfield was bombed by a host of planes including high altitude B-17s during the day and lower altitude PBY Black Cats at night. Despite almost daily bombing and strafing the buildup on Munda and New Georgia Island continued. On January 3, 1943 Admiral Halsey decided to raid Munda for purposes of bombardment as well as a diversion and cover for army landings at Lunga Roads. Nashville, along with light cruisers Helena and St. Louis and destroyers

O'Bannon and Fletcher were selected for the mission. It was believed that the rapid continuous firing capability of the cruisers six-inch guns was particularly suited for the task at hand. Task Force 67, the "Ainsworth Express" after Admiral Ainsworth, escorted and provided protection for the troop transports steaming from Espiritu Santo to Lunga Roads and then Flagship Nashville and the rest of the bombardment force headed north towards Rendova at twenty-six knots. At nightfall, with a moonless sky spotted with dark storm clouds, Nashville, Helena, and St. Louis each launched a scout plane with orders to hold a pattern away from the ships until further notice. Destroyer Fletcher led the single column while flagship Nashville was directly astern as the first cruiser. The ships slowed to eighteen knots and adjusted course slightly to maximize the firing angle. Seconds past 0100, now January 5, with fire control radars aimed at a prominent black rock, Nashville opened fire with a full salvo and was right on target and then when the task force spotter radioed "No change!" all ships let loose with salvo after salvo, sending beautiful but deadly tracers streaming through the dark sky and creating large balls of rising red and orange flame inland. The cruisers switched to "continuous rapid fire" made famous by Nashville during the Doolittle raid. Scout plane spotters radioed "Beautiful, excellent!" at the marksmanship of the Nashville, St. Louis, and Helena. Multiple secondary explosions and sky high flames attested to the devastating firepower relentlessly poured on to the Japanese facilities and troops who suffered overwhelming but indeterminable casualties. Soon thereafter, as the firing line of ships continued abreast of the island the destroyers took their turns on the firing line. Japanese return fire was light and fell short of the cruisers as the destroyers rapidly closed in on the beaches and scored direct, almost point blank hits on the Japanese batteries. Munda Airfield was hit with almost 1,400 rounds of five-inch projectiles and 3,000 rounds of six-inch shells in less than an hour (roughly one point three shells per second!) and by 0150 the column made course southeast and retired. Scout damage assessment planes the next morning reported extensive damage to Munda and a total lack of anti-aircraft fire. Once again, the continuous rapid firing capability and marksmanship of Nashville and her sister light cruisers were the scourge of the Japanese.

Nashville and the rest of the bombardment group steamed away from their target at twenty-eight knots, putting some quick distance between themselves and enemy aircraft by sunrise in reaching the south coast of Guadalcanal. The task force then reduced speed so the cruisers could recover their scout planes as Admiral Tisdale's task force rendezvoused. Recovering scout planes is an art and a science, and dangerous if under enemy attack. The ship must slow down and semi-circle to make a "slick," essentially smooth water for the plane to land on and then, slow further to an uneasy few knots to recover the plane via the stern crane. The crane lowers a wire that the pilot attaches to the plane and he and his craft are raised onto the deck. During this recovery off Guadalcanal, without any warning from the combat air patrol overhead or any ship's radar, four Japanese "Vals" dove at over 300 miles an hour out of the sun towards the ships just as the Nashville plane landed on the water and was maneuvering into position to be hoisted aboard. Almost dead still in the water, the Nashville was a sitting duck and highly vulnerable. Cruiser Honolulu had three bombs just miss her and the Australian cruiser Achilles took a direct hit on her number three turret, killing thirteen and wounding eight. The Helena knocked down one plane with a hit from the new Mark thirty-two proximity-influence fuse shell and a Navy Wildcat fighter took care of another with the remaining enemy planes hightailing it out of there. Nashville was not in a position to fire unless she was willing to risk hitting American planes, so she maneuvered violently as her best air defense. Afterwards, Nashville and the rest of the task force continued their patrol duties.

But by late January it was time for Nashville and others in the Task Force "Ainsworth Express" to hit the Japanese again. The enemy had been supplying Munda Airfield from the south via supply ships traversing Kula Gulf under cover of night, with the supplies traveling over land and the supply ships running out of harm's way by daylight. Kolombangara Island, for the most part a large volcanic cone, bordered the west side of Kula Gulf. It was here the Japanese were not only staging supplies for Munda but also building a massive 6,000 foot runway that was nearly completed by January 22.

Admiral Ainsworth's Task Force 67 composed of light cruisers Nashville, Helena, Honolulu, and St. Louis, and destroyers DeHaven, Nicholas, Radford, O'Bannon, Drayton, Lamson, and Hughes departed the New Hebrides and were trailed by unhindered Japanese scout planes since the task force was not able to raise the fighter planes of Henderson

Field for protection. But the ships did the next best thing by misleading the scouts with a feint towards Munda. However, after nightfall the task force split with cruisers Nashville and Helena and destroyers Hughes, Lamson, and Drayton continuing up the infamous Slot while the others sailed back to the south of Guadalcanal.

Unlike the bombardment raid on Munda, this was a full moon night and despite the thin overcast plenty of light was shone on the ships to make them easily visible, almost glowing as the soft moonlight reflected off their decks and superstructure. If they were spotted by scout planes the larger Japanese ships in Kula Gulf would be forewarned. As it was, just past 2400 hours two Japanese "Bettys" with full running lights engaged appeared over the task force and signaled the ships with blinker signals, most likely assuming they were Japanese and wishing to confirm identity. Admiral Ainsworth smartly chose not to respond at all rather than respond with a reply guaranteed to be incorrect. Luckily, the planes apparently were satisfied the ships were Japanese and they departed the area.

Thereafter the task force entered Kula Gulf with flagship Nashville in the third slot, again leading the cruisers, behinds destroyers O'Bannon and Nicholas. Commencing at 0200 Nashville and Helena began rapid continuous fire and relentlessly poured over 2,000 rounds of deadly six-inch shells onto the Japanese, igniting large fires and explosions on the enemy base. The destroyers added another 1,500 rounds of five-inch fire. As with Munda, Japanese return fire from coastal batteries was insignificant in number, accuracy, and effect. The moonlight filtered by the slight overcast bathed the ships in a soft but easily visible light and within thirty minutes Japanese planes dove on the task force. A rain squall provided momentary cover for the task force and radar-directed anti-aircraft fire spewed up from the sea towards the planes. No hits or near hits were made on any of the ships but it was interesting that the Japanese dropped colored flares and float flares onto the task force, creating an eerie light show, but with no effect on much of anything. Admiral Ainsworth's Nashville led Task Force 67 continued to follow Admiral Halsey's orders to "Keep pushing the Japs around."

For several months Nashville was based at Espiritu Santo where the crew had regular liberty. Joseph A. Graves SM2c decided to go on liberty for one night with the ship's band. Of course, he did not see it as a problem that he was not a member of the band, "I guess the craziest and dumbest thing I did was to let a good friend of mine talk me into going ashore with the ship's band. He played in the string band and they were playing in the Officer's Club. I took a drum and sat on the bandstand with them and got free drinks at every intermission. I don't remember getting back to the ship, but was very fortunate not to get a court martial." One wonders if Joseph attempted to play the drums at some point or simply was satisfied to sit there quietly and enjoy the free drinks. Joe Fales was assigned to build baseball and football fields and tennis courts ashore. But he also had some fun. "We'd climb coconut trees and throw down coconuts and race sand crabs." And knowing sailors and Marines, there were probably some guys betting on sand crab races somewhere on the island. After all, why would one of their favorite activities be confined to the ship? Gambling is one of a few activities that sailors seem to take to religiously, regardless that it is illegal aboard ship and that officers at times made an effort to find a well-hidden game in progress. Charles R. Conrad remembers, "A.B.Speed hiding in the dough trough in the bake shop during a raid on one of 'Turk's' crap games." He was not caught.

In Espiritu Santo Nashville continued to serve as a task force flagship and constantly patrolled the waters off the Solomons, always under threat from Japanese air and submarine forces. In fact, Nashville did so much patrolling she ran low on some supplies as Richard Metcalf stated, "we were having to do extra patrol and we ran out of supplies, our menu was pancakes, beans, beans on pancakes, and pancake rollups with beans."

Those working in the galley like Charles E. Purdue had to stretch supplies and make do with what was on hand. This was always standard procedure. When he first came aboard the young Purdue was one day making French Toast for the officers. He was conscientious with the recipe directions and added cinnamon as directed. But Purdue mistakenly grabbed the cayenne pepper instead and added it to the batter. Taste testing the batter, he was shocked into realizing his mistake. Not wanting to throw scarce supplies out, he creatively attempted to mask the flavor as best he could with sugar, cinnamon, and who knows what else. When the Captain's Orderly came to see him after breakfast and announced that the Captain wanted to see him, Purdue just knew he was headed for the brig. Reporting immediately, Purdue was relieved to hear the Captain say "Purdue, that was the best god dam French toast I ever had, what did you do?" Purdue replied, "I tried to be creative with our spices, Captain." "Well done!" replied the Captain.

Long at sea and short on supplies, Nashville got orders for a long awaited and well earned respite on March 26 and headed towards the wonderful liberty port of Sydney, Australia where she was greeted as if she had saved Australia itself when she arrived on March 31. Going into Sydney was part of the first tour of sea duty for a few of the men. Morris Short and another new sailor were on the bridge and the weather at first was a little rough as they entered Sydney harbor. The other guy got seasick and was sent below, leaving Short to handle both duties, including taking the wheel and steering the ship. "Ever steer a ship before?" Morris was asked by the officer in charge. "No sir, never even drove a car," was the honest answer of the eighteen-year-old sailor. But he learned his duty quickly, as they all did.

To this day Sydney is always mentioned by the crew whenever they speak of liberty ashore. Allan Ensor said of this first trip to Australia, "A warm welcome came from a large crowd of Aussies that greeted us on the dock. Women seemed anxious to take a Yank in tow and show us a good time. This is one battle we lost and no battle stars were issued." Some men went dancing and drinking, others sightseeing. Ron Neff and some friends decided to see the Outback and did so in an automobile powered by, of all things, charcoal. Alex Zdurne was struck by the beauty of the cathedral and park. "They had the most beautiful cathedral I have ever seen. People ate lunch in the beautiful park and when finished you couldn't even find a gum wrapper." And what can a sailor say about a city that, as Pat Carigan explains, "when you sailed into Sydney the girls in the houses would be waving their skivvies at you." Indeed, the crew was warmly welcomed and they welcomed the warmth of the Aussies.

"Sydney was great. The first time in Sydney Al Charles and I went ashore together, we had a ball. I cashed in some money at a Sydney bank and got back more money than I had room in my pockets and money belt," recalled Charles R. Conrad.

MacArthur came aboard the Nashville in Australia as he would several times during time war. He came to consider the Nashville a friend and home away from home of sorts. On one of MacArthur's visits several of the Nashville officers wanted the machine shop to make the general a pipe stand. A simple enough proposition it seemed at first thought.

But as with anything done by committee, by the military, and in war time, it was far more involved. Several officers had some sailors take Alex Zdurne MM2c, working in the machine shop at the time, on board a PT boat and then ashore once to Borneo to search for downed Japanese Zeros and other planes. Why? To get the scrap metal, specifically pieces of the propeller. One wonders how much metal is needed to make a simple pipe stand. No matter, as Alex and the propeller were dutifully brought back to Nashville. Alex went to work and soon a Japanese propeller, probably from pre-war American scrap metal to begin with, was presented to MacArthur in the form of a pipe stand. No word on how the General reacted.

Charles R. Conrad remembered, "General MacArthur had the Admiral's Cabin on the portside forward of the number four, five-inch gun so I saw him every time he was aboard. I remember seeing him on the bridge standing during our firing with plenty of cotton stuffed in his ears."

Joe Fales was not impressed with MacArthur and thought him a little on the arrogant side. "I was on the bridge when he was there once. I was a boatswain's helmsman, engine telegraph operator, and boatswain's mate of the watch, so I got to observe him quite a bit. He really just strolled up and down on the quarterdeck or the bridge and out on the wings. He walked with an air that he wanted you to be impressed with him."

By May 6 the Navy was employing new tactics in the steady war of pushing the Japanese forces around. Minelayers Prebble, Gamble, and Breese (converted old four-stack destroyers of WWI vintage) led by destroyer Radford, entered Blackett Strait off the coast of Kolombangara and commenced laying mines, always a dangerous operation. Nashville, along with light cruisers Honolulu and St. Louis and destroyers O'Bannon, Strong, Chevalier, and Taylor, headed up The Slot from Vela Gulf to block any potential Japanese surface attack on the mine laying operation. A moonless night and torrential downpour created a condition of zero visibility in the narrow strait. An environment great for providing cover from aircraft and submarines but hazardous for multiple ships operating in close quarters with deadly mines being deployed. Mine laying was successful and the brave little minelayers were escorted by Nashville and her high speed task force at such a rate of speed that the minelayers dropped out of formation at Tulagi for fuel. The mission paid off the very next day when Japanese destroyers Oyashio and Kagero fatally stuck mines, presumably with all or most hands lost.

Next up was the mining of other entrances to Kula Gulf and Admiral Halsey once again appointed Admiral Ainsworth and flagship Nashville the honor and responsibility for the operation. Very early on May 12-13 Nashville and the bombardment group and the minelayers rendezvoused in the middle of a deceptively calm sea under a clear sky. As a diversion to keep Japanese attention away from the minelayers, Nashville and friends steamed along the west coast of Kolombangara and let loose with a showy barrage on Vila Airfield, totally surprising the Japanese who were preoccupied with searchlight tracking of a PBY Black Cat overhead. Sailors on board the cruisers and destroyers could hear the sudden wailing of the Japanese warning siren as shells came crashing down on planes, men, munitions, and airfield. After fifteen minutes Nashville and most of the rest of the task force steered close to the New Georgia shore and bombarded Bairoko, the head of the new overland highway to Munda Airfield while St. Louis, Jenkins, and Fletcher bombarded Munda itself. Simultaneously, the minelayers were doing the job at the entrance to Kula Gulf and then all ships once again rendezvoused and departed the area via a mine free gap on the New Georgia side. It was another well-coordinated and successful operation.

However, the success was tempered with a serious accident aboard Nashville during the bombardment, one that cost the lives of twenty men. Not long after Nashville opened fire on Vila Airfield a premature ignition of powder charges on reportedly the 13th salvo in Turret No. 3 set off a thunderous explosion and sent a massive wall of fire down three decks under the turret, vaporizing and burning men and violently shaking the ship. Turret No. 3, manned mostly by Marines, was in continuous fire mode as were all the turrets, and a shell exploded in the loading tray prior to being rammed into the chamber. In half a second, nineteen Marines were dead. One man who survived the massive explosion, Henry Clay Pruitt FC2c, was the range finder operator. Patrick Carigan FC3c remembers, "Pruitt, whose face and eyes were shielded by the rubber mask on the rangefinder, managed to crawl out the back door of the turret and tried to crawl through the lifelines and into the sea. Luckily, he got hung up in the lifelines and was found by the men on deck assigned to clear away the empty casings. Pruitt was later removed to a hospital ship at Espiritu Santo and was saved, though he was badly disfigured. Another of his friends from "F" Division and I visited him on the Solace and he was able to talk with us. He mostly bragged about the 'angel' of a nurse who took care of him."

Charles L. Norman WT1c was a stretcher bearer in the forward battle dressing station. "We had to go topside to the turret and get the injured out of the turret through the small hatches. It was dark and the guns were still firing. The injured were badly burned, in handling them skin came off in our hands and the odor, I still remember."

Samuel Sanders S1c just escaped death. "I was put under the gun turret, as it revolved my job was to push the empty casings away so they didn't get stuck. At the last moment before we bombarded the island I was taken out because they expected an attack by air. The marine that took my place was killed along with the others."

The explosion sent Lawrence Cavanaugh, who was normally assigned to a 40 MM gun but was now picking up expended shells from the big five-inch guns, flying over the side of the ship with only his arm caught in the lifelines holding his unconscious body a few feet above the seas as Nashville cut through the water at high speed. As he slowly regained consciousness Cavanaugh noticed the screams and groans of the wounded and dieing. But hear was all he could do for he could not see and thought he was now blind. He laboriously pulled himself up over the lifeline only to get knocked down again by something in the dark, possibly a loose shell. He was taken down to Sick Bay and eventually made his way to Oak Knoll Naval Hospital and a lengthy physical therapy before being assigned to a destroyer in the Atlantic and getting dive bombed by German Stukas while passing through the Straits of Gibraltar.

Heroism was common. Among others, Lester Lindsey Morton S1c received a Commendation for his actions after the turret exploded. Stationed in the forward battle dressing station the young Morton unhesitatingly entered the horror of the turret and cared for the wounded as noted by the commendation "in a highly efficient manner for many hours afterward continued to perform his duties in a highly meritorious manner assuming more responsibility and accomplishing more in the care of the wounded than could normally have been expected..." Sailors and Marines alike were burned about their hands, arms, and faces as they rushed to the hatches and opened them to save their crewmates. More were burned as they entered the turret in an immediate rescue attempt. They never hesitated, never faltered.

The Marines in the handling room saved the magazine and untold number of other lives by immediately flooding it. If they had not done so, the potential resultant explosion and loss of life would have been tremendous and certainly would have taken Nashville out of the war temporarily, if not permanently.

Despite the shock of the explosion and the horror of the dead and wounded, Nashville never wavered for a second in her mission and continued to carry out her orders as issued throughout the night.

Nashville returned to Espiritu Santo on May 14 where her dead and seriously wounded, including Henry Clay Pruitt, were gently removed with many a sailor and marine lining the decks and watching the somber operation. Nashville set course for San Francisco and departed Espiritu Santo on May 22, 1943 and arrived at Mare Island Naval Shipyard, her Doolittle Raid supply base, in Vallejo at the northernmost part of San Francisco Bay on June 4. She had been away for over fourteen months, at various assignments across the Pacific. In those fourteen months the crew saw plenty of action, grew older and more mature, some died, some were wounded, and the war went on even as the world continued to change. As Nashville approached the Golden Gate Bridge she was flying her Homeward Bound pennant signifying she had been gone over twelve consecutive months. Allan Ensor BM1c was aboard. "The morning of our return the signalman streamed the Homeward Bound Pennant from the mainmast, almost reaching the stern and twenty-four inches wide. The top color was red and the bottom color white, with a blue field next to the hoist. Before we came into site of the Golden Gate Bridge we received a big welcome home from a greeter we had never seen before. It dipped its wings as it made a low level pass, climbed, did a rollover, and made another low level pass dipping its wings on its return. The pilot must have been saying 'Welcome home guys, how do you like my new toy?' It was possibly a new Bell Shooting Star aircraft. The jet age was born while we were gone."

At Mare Island, where an amazing 100,000 workers repaired and built ships twenty-four noisy hours a day, seven productive days a week, Nashville not only had repairs done on Turret No.3 but also received an extensive modernization overhaul from bow to stern. It took two months, but when finished she was once again one of the most modern ships in the Navy. More importantly, she was more powerful and deadly than ever. During the modernization overhaul many men were granted liberty of one length or another and one was Patrick Carigan, who received ten days. Patrick decided to go home to see his mother. It was a noble and proper act befitting Patrick's character. But home was Liberty, Kentucky, many miles and seemingly endless, crowded train hours from Mare Island. "I spent four days each direction on the train and spent a day and a half home at most." But it was a day and a half cherished by Patrick and his family. Just fresh back at Mare Island, Patrick was assigned the unenviable Shore Patrol Duty. "I had to pull SP duty on Georgia Street in Vallejo. That was a pretty tough street because most of the sailors and Marines had come back from Guadalcanal and they were wild, wild, and trying to keep control there was a hairy job." Marine Corporal Don R. Hill summed it up, "Lower Georgia Street had two places of business, one was bars. I can't remember the second but ask a sailor, they were always pouring out of them." Delbert Ford of R Division also had Vallejo duty ashore as an SP. "The patrol hours were 1600 to 0200 or later if the Senior Patrol Officer required you. We had to sleep in the barracks at Mare Island. Part of the time we had to work with the Vallejo Police Department officers. No comment on what I thought of them." Vallejo had been a tough town ever since it became a naval base after the Civil War, but with the influx of scores of thousands of shipyard workers from across the country and thousands of battle-hardened Marines and sailors fresh from the butchery of warfare in the Pacific, her available vices were magnified accordingly. Vallejo's reputation as a tough navy town of whorehouses, bars, drunks, and fights was earned and accurate. Some sailors went to Richmond, a beehive of Liberty ship building and a little south of Vallejo and perhaps, even a little rougher. There were fights and drinking and more fights and more drinking, at least for some of the crew.

Joe Fales came back from liberty and could hardly recognize the ship. "The topside had been practically stripped away; they had been doing everything to it." But soon Joe was in the hospital for ten days having his tonsils removed. "When I came back, I was assigned a watch up in the officer's quarters and it was a fire watch. I was to sit with a welder while they welded. There was a fire extinguisher there and when it started to burn I was to put the fire out. Well, I was amazed when the welder finally pulled the mask back, it was a woman welder. And let me tell you, she was all business, she really worked hard to get everything done." At about the same time, on the opposite coast in Baltimore, George Bustin's future wife, fourteen-year-old Kathleen Hellams was welding airplane frames in the Glenn L. Martin aircraft factory. Rosie the Riveter was no myth and was working hard to win the war.

George L. Bustin, a local boy from Oakland, did not get to see his family the last time Nashville was at Mare Island in early 1942 as they loaded up for the Doolittle Raid. This time he did get liberty and saw his mom Mae and sisters Evelyn, Lorraine, and Haidee, filling up on home cooking and family love. There were more than a few locals on board Nashville who took to their homes as soon as their liberty orders were issued.

Even with over 100,000 workers and thousands of sailors and marines buzzing about, it seemed impossible that anyone would come across someone they knew, but Albert Gaines did. Albert was going about his business on deck and thought he heard his name, then again heard it in a different voice and looked up to see a man and his brother-in-law from his home town of Denver calling out to him. It was the briefest of reunion conversations but it was a tangible reminder of home for Albert.

While at Mare Island most men were still stationed aboard for duties and sleeping quarters. And while they were called sleeping quarters, not much sleeping was done. The reconstruction and construction of ships throughout Mare Island, to say nothing of the same on Nashville, never stopped. Not at night and not on Sunday. The scrapping, hammering, welding, banging, blasting, bolting, and cutting was incessant and unrelenting. No one at any time ever had a good night's sleep. "The noise was deafening day and night," said Rufus B. Thompson, Lt. Colonel USMC, "almost impossible to walk on deck and through passageways. Nights that I had duty it was near impossible to sleep when off Watch."

With modernization complete and liberty expired, it was soon time for the crew to head back into the uncertain future of war. On August 6 families, friends, and lovers said a worrisome good-bye and Nashville and new destroyer USS Trathen sailed under the foggy Golden Gate Bridge and set course for Pearl Harbor. The ships crossed the Pacific without encountering the enemy and arrived safely in Pearl Harbor on August 12, 1943. But soon enough crew and ship were once more bound for harm's way.

On August 23 Rear Admiral Charles A. Pownall's large carrier-led task force departed Pearl Harbor, with Nashville providing part of the inner protective screen for the valuable yet vulnerable carriers. As many times before and as it seems it would always be, Nashville was on a secret raid and would catch the Japanese by complete surprise.

As the sun rose on Marcus Island, September 1, Nashville's crew stood at battle stations and the carrier planes, Avengers, Wildcats, and Tomcats took off to bomb and strafe Japanese positions on the island. The surprise attack was a complete success as 80% of Japanese installations on the island were destroyed with but a loss of two fighters and one torpedo plane for the task force. The ships then set sail back to Pearl Harbor after the last aerial mission and arrived on September 8. The Japanese still held most of the strategic Solomon Islands-New Guinea area but the US Navy was indeed starting to push the Japanese harder and harder. In September Japanese Imperial Headquarters sent an urgent message: "Make every effort to hold the important southeastern area extending eastward from the eastern part of New Guinea to the Solomon Islands by repulsing all enemy attacks in that area." The Americans were coming again to push the Japanese out and the Japanese were determined to stay put. Of such things battles are created.

Nashville left Pearl Harbor again in October as part of a task force under Rear Admiral Alfred E. Montgomery, part of a quick surprise raid against Wake Island. At a brilliant red dawn on October 5, Nashville and other big-gunned ships unleashed a powerful and accurate onslaught of high explosive shells on the Japanese garrison, knocking out most of their anti-aircraft weapons, killing hundreds of troops and neutralizing their air capabilities. Follow-up bombing by unmolested Army B-24 Liberators encountered weak opposition and not a single aircraft was lost in the low-altitude mission. Carrier planes followed up on October 6 with further sorties against the stunned Japanese defenders. The raiding task force returned to Pearl Harbor, another job well done.

After a quick replenishment at Pearl Harbor, on October 19, 1943 Nashville departed and sailed to Espiritu Santo, arriving without incident on October 25. It was here that writer James Michener spent time during the war and was so impressed by the beauty around him that he was inspired to write *Tales of the South Pacific*. Albert Gaines WT1c had the opportunity to pursue an unusual hobby while the ship spent time at Espiritu Santo, "While there I used my spare time going ashore to pick up live shells. The ocean depth for considerable distance was only two feet and made wading ideal for my shell harvesting. The area had flat rocks that were only five to seven pounds weight and beneath same were the shells that had a bright circle orange on top and the size of a dime coin. I carried a two gallon galvanized bucket to keep the shells in and when I returned to the ship I used a steam hose in the boiler fire room to dissolve and clean out the creature that lived in the shell. It took a short time for a stench to come from the shells if you waited to get this creature from inside the shell. A shipmate friend that worked with our dentist supplied me with solver wire. From the wire I made connectors similar to that of a key chain and threaded a wire through each shell where I had taken a pistol drill and made holes through each shell with enough wire at each end of the shell to make a connector. I made many sets containing necklaces, bracelets, ear bobs, and sold some to shipmates to mail home to loved ones. I don't think many shipmates had my patience required to complete a shell necklace. The greatest requirement I had was access to the steam hose."

For the next few months ship and crew would be on constant duty, patrolling and bombarding day and night, constantly surprising the Japanese and fulfilling the orders to "push the Japs around" and doing all the things sailors and marines do on a warship: read, write letters to loved ones, play cards, do laundry, paint and repaint the ship, have boxing contests, and the hundreds of other routine exercises sailors do even in the middle of a war zone.

On November 3, 1943, at 0900 hours, off of Rendova, Nashville and destroyer Pringle were dispatched from the waters of Guadalcanal and rendezvoused with Task Force 39, just out of the intensive air-sea Battle of Empress Augusta Bay, and relieved the group of escort duty for four transports that had unloaded troops at Empress Augusta Bay. Nashville covered the Marine invasion on Bougainville and helped repulse a dangerous Japanese naval force with her anti-aircraft guns and clever maneuvering. At times the local natives, who detested the Japanese due to their harsh treatment, were helpful not only to the Army and Marines ashore who had invaded the islands, but to the Navy as well. Eddie Yusko saw it for himself. "The natives would kill and roast a pig near the Japanese positions, making sure there was a lot of smoke visible at sea, alerting the Nashville and supporting ships as the their locations. The Navy would wait a day for the natives to feast and then move their families safely away and then start a bombardment of the Japs." It was the South Seas version of smoke signals and it was effective. Many of the Japanese that escaped the Nashville bombardments fell prey to native anger and became shrunken heads displayed in the villages.

Nashville spent Christmas 1943 with a warm turkey meal for the crew and no action, and then on December 26 she provided more bombardment support in the form of shelling Cape Gloucester, New Britain for that strongly opposed invasion. The shelling began at dawn in conjunction with sister ship Phoenix and Australian cruisers Australia and Shropshire along with destroyers Warramunda and Arunta. Nashville expended 728 rounds of main battery shells accurately hitting the airstrip, fuel, and ammo dumps and shore batteries along with the usual unknown number of Japanese troops, eliminating some of the firepower the invading allied forces would face and saving incalculable numbers of Allied lives. The ship and crew had become one in these bombardments, functioning smoothly, efficiently, and unfortunately for the enemy, deadly.

This routine of escort duty, invasion cover and bombardment and surprise close range shelling of enemy airfields and positions on many islands continued almost unabated for many months. On February 29, 1944 Nashville and sister ship Phoenix continued the practice of the devastating shelling of Japanese positions, this time on the Admiralty Islands as the latest invasion began, once again hitting an airstrip, fuel, and ammo depots and countless Japanese troops. By now, Nashville had been the scourge of the Japanese army and navy for most of the war.

On March 4 Nashville, Phoenix, and HMAS Shropshire rained shells down on Japanese positions on Hauwei Island that were posing a danger to supply landings. They soon posed a danger no longer. On

March 7 Nashville expertly shelled the island once again to eliminate the last hiding Japanese gun positions. Such enemy positions were totally eliminated, ceasing to function or exist.

Part of General MacArthur's baggage

Officers on deck, April 19, 1944

The Nashville band in Sydney, Australia

The Nashville band, again in Sydney

The swinging Nashville band

Not an unusual scene for Nashville liberty ashore

CHAPTER 6
War in the Pacific: More Islands

***

"The Navy didn't support us, they saved our necks!"

-General Swift, US Army

***

Admiralty Islands (January-February 44)

General MacArthur, as part of his "island-hopping" strategy, had decided it was not necessary to tackle the 100,000 plus Japanese troops at Rabaul head on, but rather they could be isolated and minimized and the road to Tokyo taken a step closer to goal by bypassing Rabaul and occupying the Admiralty Islands for a much needed forward base. If the US could hold the Admiralty Islands with large land, air, and naval facilities, then the Allies could control a good thousand square miles of Pacific territory that included Biak, Truk, Bouganville, and the Palaus, all vital to supreme war strategy.

The Japanese had occupied the Admiralties in 1942 and built airfields on Los Negros (Momote Field) and at Seeadler Harbor (Lorengau Field) the next year. There were less than an estimated 5,000 Japanese soldiers on the islands. Early and incomplete photorecon intelligence had indicated the Japanese may have pulled out of the islands completely. In fact, Japanese troops were staying completely out of sight during the day and did not fire on low flying Allied aircraft. Later intelligence indicated there were still Japanese present so it was decided to do a "reconnaissance in force." Nashville and sister ship Phoenix along with destroyers Beale, Hutchins, Daly, and Bache, under command of Admiral Berkey, were ordered to cover the approach of the landing force as well as provide any required bombardment of the island. Nashville, Phoenix, and the destroyers sailed from Cape Sudest, New Guinea at 1600 hours on February 27, 1944, leading by roughly eleven miles the landing forces trailing securely in formation. They arrived off Hyane Harbor a little past 0700, escaping detection by the Japanese.

At 0723 the order was given, "Deploy," and the landings commenced. Landing craft debarked, 3 B-24 Army Liberators dropped bombs (the only aircraft to make it through the rough weather) and at 0740 the destroyers started a barrage on specific targets. Soon machine gun fire rang out from Japanese positions ashore and large guns lobbed salvos at Nashville and Phoenix but did not find the mark. It was a deadly mistake for the Japanese gunners. Nashville and Phoenix immediately and simultaneously returned fire and hit and destroyed a large naval gun with only the third shot, duly impressing General MacArthur who, along with Admiral Kinkaid was observing aboard Phoenix. The landings went well and Momote Airfield, abandoned, was taken by 0950. There were now 1,000 troops ashore with an estimated 2,000 Japanese opposing them. More extensive and tough fighting was ahead but the initial operation was a success. On March 2, Task Force 74, under the command of Rear Admiral Crutchley of the Royal Navy and including Nashville, Phoenix, HMAS Shropshire, and four destroyers, sailed past Cape Sudest, New Guinea and began a patrol that covered the area between the Equator and the Admiralty Islands. Nashville and the other ships of the task force maintained this patrol through March 7 except when horrendous weather or bombardment of Japanese positions interrupted the routine. The Allies had control of the Admiralty Island by April 3, 1944.

As often as the branches of military service are in contention with each other in terms of strategy, tactics, credit, and publicity, they do in fact work well together for the common good and in a way not generally matched by other nations during the war. While the Japanese struggled the entire war for a semblance of interservice cooperation, more important in this war than in any in history, the United States, in the words of one Japanese naval officer, "attained perfection in such cooperation." In this operation the support of the Navy was magnanimously acknowledged by Army General Swift in his post-battle report. He stated, "The bald statement, 'The naval forces supported the action,' appearing in the chronology, is indeed a masterpiece of understatement. When asked regarding the effect of naval gunfire support the commanding general of one brigade made the laconic reply, 'The Navy didn't support us, they saved our necks!' All commanders firmly believe that, especially during the initial phases, the balance of war was tipped in our favor by the superb support rendered by the naval forces. The bulk of the naval force moved to the south (referring to Nashville and Phoenix). From these positions they laid a heavy barrage on the enemy positions. So cleverly was this barrage placed and so devastating its effect that the Japs were forced out of their positions right into the waiting bands of automatic fire of the dismounted cavalrymen. 'The Naval forces supported the action.' Indeed! Without the Navy there would not have been any action." Once again, Nashville and her Navy brothers had done their part towards the final victory. Japanese Admiral Ugaki noted in his diary, "The swiftness of the enemy offenses are making all our sluggish countermeasures abortive... the enemy's present strength is just like a raging fire, so irresistible that a small amount of water cannot put it out."

***

Hollandia (April-June 44)

Early in 1942 the Japanese invaded the northern coast of the near prehistoric island of New Guinea, but did not succeed in taking complete control of one of the largest Pacific islands. For a couple of years the Japanese garrison never had to deal with the Allies and were left alone to build up bases and gun positions, fighting only the hostile environment and unfriendly natives at times. But by early 1944, Allied forces had come ever closer by way of successful sea, air, and land battles for Papua, the Admiralties, Rabaul, and western New Britain. The western part of the island of New Guinea, known as Dutch New Guinea, populated by Stone Age peoples surviving in unforgiving jungle terrain, had but one good sheltered harbor, Humboldt Bay. The bay and surrounding area came to be known to the Americans after a small village in the area, Hollandia. The Japanese had laboriously constructed three airfields on the island and were working on a fourth in early 1944, at Tami. Since the nearest American air field was 500 miles away it was necessary to construct a base closer to any Hollandia operations. Detailed plans for the Navy part of the operation were determined at a meeting of Admiral Nimitz and staff at Brisbane, Australia, March 25-26. MacArthur's army already had plans to invade in three locations (Tanahmerah Bay, Humboldt Bay, and Aitape) on April 22.

The Japanese had plans to develop Hollandia into a major base of offensive operations against the American fleet, sort of an offensive line of defense they were building around western Dutch New Guinea, the Marianas, Netherlands East Indies, and the Palaus, but continued Allied offensive operations had pushed back the Hollandia part of the execution. So the Japanese poured much men and material into New Guinea as a revised line of defensive and offensive operations.

Hollandia was the next stage of the strategy of island hopping by the Allies. The Japanese hated but respected this strategy but were helpless to prevent it. "This was the type of strategy we hated most," said a senior intelligence officer of the Japanese Eighth Area Army after the war. "The Americans, with minimal losses, attacked and seized a relatively weak area, constructed airfields, and then proceeded to cut the supply lines to troops in that area. Without engaging in a large scale operation, our strong points were gradually starved out. The Japanese Army preferred direct assault, after the German fashion, but the Americans flowed into our weaker points and submerged us, just as water seeks the weakest entry to sink a ship. We respected this type of strategy for its brilliance because it gained the most while losing the least." While "weak area" is certainly open to interpretation and relativity, as Biak would prove to be a deadly and costly assault, more formidable targets like the Japanese base at Truk were in fact bombed and bypassed for the most part until the inevitable major assaults on the Philippines, Iwo Jima, and Okinawa.

The Navy had caught an intelligence break in March of 1944 that would directly affect their operations at Hollandia and even more so in the Philippines in June. There were powerful Japanese naval units within a day or so striking distance of Biak but it was determined that they would most likely not commit themselves entirely unless they were sure of the battle location and conditions. Navy codebreakers at Pearl Harbor knew that Admiral Koga, who succeeded Admiral Yamamoto after Army P-38s shot him out of the sky (also a result of codebreaking intelligence), was killed in an airplane crash on Cebu, Philippines, and his chief of staff Vice Admiral Fukudome was captured by Philippine guerillas. Fukudome carried a briefcase that held the secret plans of "Zebra Order," a plan for a decisive battle (as all Japanese plans stubbornly and fatally tended to be) against the US Navy, in range of land-based aircraft, thus not risking what was left of Japan's carriers and irreplaceable carrier pilots.

The Navy had three attack groups for the invasion: Western Attack Group (Tanahmerah Bay), Central Attack Group (Humboldt Bay), and Eastern Attack Group (Aitape). For those Nashville crewmen who at times complained they had to be in two places at one time, this time they were correct. Nashville, requested by MacArthur to serve as his flagship, was to be at both Tanahmerah Bay and Aitape. Allan D. Ensor was given the duty of piping the General aboard, much to his surprise. "I noticed Chief Boatswain's mate 'Foxy' Chambers heading toward me at an unusual fast pace. 'Ensor, get into your dress uniform,' he said. 'You will be piping General MacArthur aboard at 1000. Eight side boys will meet you at the Quarterdeck at 0930,' he said quickly as he turned and headed forward again. 'Aye aye Chief,' was all I could say as the thought of 'why me?' raced through my mind. After a few practice calls on my boatswain's pipe, I changed into a dress uniform and reported to the Quarterdeck and found the side boys already there. I told them we would be providing side honors for General MacArthur who would be coming alongside in a motor torpedo boat. After stationing the side boys in two ranks facing each other to form a passageway, I instructed them when to begin their salute. Several practice sessions were made. As the PT boat approached, I piped it alongside. Long, rolling swells caused the General a little difficulty in reaching the bottom platform of the gangway, but he managed to step on at the right moment. I started my piping and managed to hold the call until he passed through the two rows of saluting side boys. Returning the salute, he was then greeted by the Commanding Officer. Photographers were stationed in the superstructure to record this historic event." One of those photographers, who would take hundreds of photographs of the General over time, was Nashville crewman Joe Mills. MacArthur had flown to Finschhafen in his personal B-17, which he had aptly named *Bataan*. The media people had also come along on the plane. The circus had begun.

Rufus B. Thompson Lt. Colonel USMC was in charge of the General's security while he was aboard the ship. "When the General and his staff first came aboard I had a Marine orderly posted at his cabin. An Army colonel told me the Chief of Staff wanted to see me." The Chief of Staff questioned Rufus about the posting of the Marine orderly and after he talked with MacArthur Rufus was told the General wanted to see him. "After he said something about didn't I think the Army orderlies would do, I told him my Marines were acquainted with the ship, communications center, battle stations, evacuation and abandon ship stations, etc. Also that it was my duty to provide protection for all flag officers on board. He accepted it and every time he was on board a Marine served as his orderly. Also, four Marines accompanied him ashore on every occasion when he was aboard." And most of the time Joe Mills made those trips and took photographs.

The task force, of which Nashville was the flagship, included eight jeep carriers and sailed toward Hollandia in a roundabout and deceptive route to mask the location of the intended invasion target. At times some people referred to the 7th Fleet as MacArthur's Navy, and not without a hint of derision. The 7th was to carry MacArthur frequently on his island hopping campaign across the southern Pacific while Nimitz's fast carriers and the Marines relentlessly attacked the Japanese through the Central Pacific.

A brilliant plan of deception was put into play days before D-Day. Intending to make the Japanese believe that the next target was Hansa Bay-Wewak and not Hollandia, false invasion plans were leaked in pieces. Dummy paratroopers were dropped, subs dropped off empty rubber boats on shore, and photoreconnaissance planes swooped over the area as if part of a standard invasion preparation. The Army did not bomb, at least not in a normal pre-invasion manner, anything near Hollandia. The intent was to lull the Japanese into thinking Hollandia was definitely not to be the target of an invasion. The ruse was 100% successful. Late March and on April 3 the Army flew massive surprise raids against Hollandia. The entire Japanese air force of up to 400 planes, along with supporting fuel and supply dumps, was totally destroyed!

With MacArthur aboard, Nashville arrived at Tanahmerah Bay 1320 hours on D-Day itself. A high level meeting of General Krueger, General Eichelberger, and Admiral Barbey occurred while they all enjoyed the Nashville's vanilla and Coke ice cream sodas, and then left the ship at 1500 hours to go ashore for a closer look at the situation. Within an hour and a half they returned to their respective ships, MacArthur returning to Nashville to travel to Aitape the next day, but not before he returned ashore again for an hour.

The attack by Nashville and other ships and the aforementioned Army air force completely surprised the Japanese. The Japanese army in New Guinea had anticipated an invasion to the east of Hollandia, at Hansa Bay. They had been completely deceived and as a result their air force was annihilated on the ground, their facilities and support structures utterly destroyed and a good many of their ground forces blasted into small pieces by naval gunfire and so, after a token resistance, they fled inland under cover of the jungle.

MacArthur used Nashville on three occasions as his flagship, she was known as his favorite of all the ships he had temporarily set up headquarters on which is most likely why he chose Nashville for his return to the Philippines and reportedly had plans to use her for the later surrender ceremonies in Tokyo Bay itself. When MacArthur and staff came aboard, or whenever any flag rank officer and staff came aboard, some of the Nashville crew had to give up their quarters temporarily. This was not necessarily the problem one might think it to be. Richard A. Smith FC3c did not mind at all. "We often had to give up our bunks to flag staff, but I usually slept on deck under a six-inch gun turret, so I didn't mind."

Before Nashville reached Australia, MacArthur, emboldened by the latest success and ever in a hurry to reach the Philippines, proposed an immediate jump forward of 125 miles to Wakde-Sarmi. Despite some resistance by his staff, by the time Nashville reached Australia, MacArthur had ordered the invasion of Wakde, and so it was. Nashville eased into the dock at Sydney for a well-earned and overdue delightful ten day stay for the crew.

Be it their first Sydney liberty or not, the crew loved the city and the people. Allan Ensor BM1c had enjoyed his first liberty in Sydney and was sure he would enjoy his second. "During a second cruise to Sydney," Ensor stated, "two incidents could have had an adverse affect on my physical well-being and career. Ski, a 2nd Division BM1c, and I were sitting in a park 'charting our course' when four Australian soldiers approached us removing their belts that had a large buckle. It was very evident what they intended to do but we held our ground. And then an unexpected event took place. Two Navy Shore Patrolmen came over the top of a small bridge close to where we were sitting. When sighting the shore patrolmen the soldiers changed their direction and replaced their belts.

No bumps, no bruises, no broken bones thanks to the shore patrolman."
But there was to be more, in this case, self-imposed adventure for Allan
Ensor. "The last day of liberty several other deck petty officers and I
decided to play it dangerously. With liberty about to expire we decided
to drink a sack full of beer we still had. We decided to go aboard after
the morning lines had been singled up, even though we knew we would
be AWOL. This was not a good idea! After consuming several bottles we
noticed a crane moving in position to remove gangplank to the ship. We
dropped everything and ran to the ship barely in time to make it aboard.
Luckily, all we received at Captain's Mast was a good chewing out and
reminded of the consequences had we missed the ship's movement."

J.D. Buddy Baccus had great liberties in Australia and summed it
up succinctly yet accurately, "Liberty, well I was very young and the best
was in Australia."

Patrick Carigan of F Division certainly had a good time in Sydney
and apparently so did most of his buddies. "I was fortunate enough to
have lots of money going into port, having cleaned out a crap game in the
Optical Shop the night before our arrival. The losers that night included
all of my best friends. I tried my best to make sure they all had some
fun in Sydney as I rented an entire floor in a small hotel the first night
and engaged a taxi and driver to stay available to all of us for our entire
stay. We had a Ship's Dance that first night and when the last waltz was
played I found Bill Rudman FC1c and I had two Aussie daisies in tow
and our Executive Officer was so stoned he didn't know his name. Bill
and I commandeered a flat bed truck to haul us back to our hotel, with
the daisies in the cab and Bill and I holding the helpless commander
secure on the open flatbed. When the commander woke up in my bed
the next morning, he was shamefaced but very grateful. When he got
back to the ship he told his Yeoman to be sure my liberty card came out
every day. As far as I know, old 'Joe Pot' (me) was the only enlisted man
on the Nashville to be accorded that honor. I spent every dollar of my
winnings on booze and rooms for my F Division buddies."

With a strong destroyer escort the battle-hardened ship and men
slipped out of Sydney Harbor and sailed to Milne Bay where she anchored
at New Guinea's southwestern tip, awaiting further orders and no doubt,
battle action. While anchored at Milne Bay Rufus B. Thompson and
a Marine detachment went ashore "for rifle and pistol practice at an

old Japanese rifle range," remembered Rufus. "I saw a group of natives coming down a hillside through the low brush and trees. The leader, no doubt the chief, was a tall, dignified person wearing a formal tails jacket and an Abe Lincoln stovepipe hat and using a long staff. Following him were about six or eight women and children. The women had large bundles on their heads and clad only in some kind of loin cloth or skirt. What a picture that would have been." The Marines were treated royally, no doubt in appreciation for driving the hated Japanese from the area. Natives in New Guinea and other Pacific islands hated the Japanese for their harsh and murderous treatment and in return, they eventually preyed upon the Japanese, often beheading them.

At 0600 on April 22 Nashville and light cruisers Phoenix and Boise let loose with both six-inch and five-inch batteries at designated targets on Hollandia and surrounding areas. Salvo, after deadly salvo was fired for half an hour before the destroyers, closer to shore in shallower water, took over with their own point blank bombardment. The combined shelling entailed 3,700 rounds of five-inch and 1,600 rounds of six-inch shells. Just before 1000 hours General MacArthur disembarked from Nashville for a look-see on the invasion beach.

American success seemed inevitable and Hollandia was taken. Eventually, even though there were still remnants of deadly Japanese resistance on New Guinea near Hollandia, liberty was granted to the crews of navy ships, including Nashville. Far different than the bars and adoring women of modern Sydney, liberty on such recently taken and facilities-challenged islands usually took the form of a few hours on the beach with two warm beers per man and a softball game against Marines, Army, Navy or your own crews. Sometimes, sailors wanted a little more and let their youthful curiosity drive their decisions. Such was the case with Robert L. Shafer of the Lookout Division and four of his buddies.

Robert remembers fondly that "it was a day for some R&R; the liberty boat was headed to the island so the crew could drink their usual two beers and have a softball game in the hot sun. John had another idea, why don't they go into the jungle nearby and find some wild limes, take them back, find some ice, and make limeade. This sounded like a really good idea so they went, Shafer, Stalls, Todd, Byrd, and Kyler headed into the jungle."

"It didn't take ten minutes to lose sight of the sun as they soon stumbled over the large bamboo branches cutting them with their sharp edges. Suddenly John knew the boys were completely lost. At first they nearly panicked not knowing what to do. As usual, John kept his head and remembered that there was a Marine camp on the island, located on a river. All they had to do was find the river, follow it to the Marine base and back to the beach. Well, there was only one problem, where was the river?

As they stumbled along, Byrd put his foot through the thick vegetation he was walking on and into the river he dropped. It seems that they were walking over the river and didn't even know it. This solved one problem. They only had to follow it in the right direction.

Soon, by luck more than survival skills, they came into a clearing, and just across the clearing was the Marine base. Everybody stripped down to their skivvies and got ready to swim across. Two of the sailors sheepishly put up their hands and admitted they couldn't swim. John at first was mad but after screaming at the two, he calmed down. This was really no problem; they would find a log and put the two non-swimmers and their clothes on the log. There was only one problem. As the gang was pushing the log out into the river, it ran into a current in the middle and the pushing began to get tricky. Suddenly, the log rolled over scattering the two non-swimmers and all of their clothes into the river.

Now there was a real problem as the boys were floundering around trying to stay afloat and down the river went all of the clothes. Naturally the first thing for the others was to save their buddies so they grabbed and shoved them back onto the log. By the time this was done everyone's clothes were long gone down the river.

The Marines helped them out of the river so there they were, standing in their skivvies. Of course, they really got kidded by the Marines who also took pity and gave them some castoff clothes, mostly too big for them, but better than nothing. Now they were only about a mile back up the river from the beach and a ride back to the ship.

They sheepishly slipped aboard the returning liberty boat and started back to the ship, but as luck would have it a big rain squall came up and everyone got soaked. At the ship, when they came up, the officer of the deck took one look and couldn't believe his eyes, six sailors dressed in Marine castoff clothes soaked, cuts around their faces and arms, and out of uniform. He knew this was one for the books, shook his head, grinned, and said all get below.

John told his buddies that night, if he ever suggested any other excursions in the jungle, get someone to shoot him. It could have really been tragic but I guess someone was watching over them. The rumor was that at night, the head hunters came down from the hills in search of Japs which they hated."

Richard Metcalf remembers the warm beer party on the beach, but also the loading of supplies by hand walking up the gangplank, which had its own bit of humor. "While carrying lime juice on our shoulders two arms would reach out the galley porthole and the crate of lime juice would disappear." The sailors that went lime hunting in the jungle probably did not know lime juice was going to be loaded at Hollandia.

J.D. Baccus was once in charge of dispensing the beer on the island. "It was in cardboard cases, I would keep a few cans in each case and give it to one of my buddies, he would take it into the jungle. After I was finished my crew and I went to the stash and got smashed. When we returned to the ship we would grab one of our buddies and throw him overboard and then scream, 'man overboard!' and jump in to save him. The Captain finally made us stop."

Beer was not the only alcohol available to the crew. An unsubstantiated but widely confirmed rumor was that the head cook had something brewing deep in the boughs of the ship, something officers could smell when they opened a specific hatch, but did not ever go deep down the steep ladders to investigate. Apparently the product of this effort was stored in some of the "water" containers of the life rafts. Luckily, neither the rafts nor the "water" was ever needed. It is assumed the concoction was at times consumed accordingly.

In a ceremony with less pomp and circumstance than normally done in peacetime or for locations safely from the battlelines, on April 25, 1944 Captain Spanagel congratulated his successor, Captain Charles Edward Coney as he was relieved of command and transferred to other duty. The well-maintained ship and highly trained and battle-tested crew took it all in stride and continued on as before.

***

Wadke-Sarmi
(May 1944)

The Wadke-Sarmi area of Dutch New Guinea was invaded by the Japanese in 1942 and they promptly built a modern aircraft runway, surfaced with crushed coral. Wadke-Sarmi lies 120 miles west of Hollandia along the north coast of the island. There are a number of small islands in the area including two by the name of Wadke. It was to be yet the latest in the many stepping stones to the eventual invasion of Japan and the end of the war.

In mid May, Nashville and the other veteran cruisers under Admirals Crutchley and Berkey departed Seeadler Harbor and assembled off Hollandia, ready to escort landing forces and bombard Wadke. Nashville and the rest of Task Force 75 had already raided and bombarded the Wadke and Biak areas on the night of April 29. Shortly after sunset on May 16, 1944 the fleet of cruisers, support ships, troop transports, and various other vessels sailed toward their latest destiny, Wadke, a mere 120 miles away. The almost 11,000 Japanese troops under the command of Lieutenant General Tagami were soon to be completely and unpleasantly surprised.

The ships stole silently in the night of a bright moon and roving tropical rainstorms. At 0600, before sunrise, the bombardment commenced with Admiral Berkey's task force of Nashville, Phoenix, and Boise raining deadly six-inch fire on Wadke, aiming for Japanese gun emplacements and Admiral Crutchley's group pounding inland targets at Sarmi and Sawar. The accompanying destroyers hit coastal targets in the bay. For several minutes the bombardment pounded the Japanese relentlessly. A halt was called to allow for aerial observation and then troop landings at the mainland beach. As soon as the troops hit the beach Nashville, Phoenix, and Boise poured a stream of six-inch salvos into Wadke Island itself. Spotter planes directed the cruisers to numerous choice targets, from fuel depots to machines gun nests. Each and every target given to Nashville was quickly hit and eliminated as the ship fired 530 five-inch rounds and 520 six-inch rounds. The spotter pilot reported "right on the ball" regarding fire accuracy. The cruisers then left the bombardment to destroyers Trathen and Beale so they could move further offshore to guard against any Japanese naval activity. Wadke was in Allied hands within a couple of days. Only four Japanese were taken prisoner, all others died for Emperor Hirohito. On the mainland the Allies had control by September. The Philippines loomed ever closer but first another island, Biak, had to be taken from its current unwelcome occupants.

General MacArthur boarding April 19, 1944, New Guinea

General MacArthur boarding

Crew playing football on the beach of Manus, Admiralty Islands

A quick respite, more football on the beach, Admiralty Islands

Two warm beers per man, September 1943

Tom O'Laughlin, Deacon Daniels, Joe Berry, Ira Bonnett, Jack Lowenbien, "Jester" Wilson, Herby Williams, C. Kenny

CHAPTER 7
Biak: Near Miss Nearly Hit

***

"There was the explosion, the ship shuddered and I'm thinking, here we go swimming."
-James Clark

***

BIAK (June 1944)

Fresh off the planning board after Wadke was Biak, the outer of two islands off the northeast coast of Geelvink Bay, scheduled for a mere ten days later. Biak, mostly a low, thick jungle plateau but with rows of limestone ridges, is forty-five miles long and twenty miles wide, has an extensive coral reef, but no natural harbors. Since the twenty-first of May, the Japanese had suspected Biak would be invaded at any moment. Aerial bombing and shore bombardment followed to confirm Japanese thinking. Admiral Ugaki had told his staff "it is absolutely necessary to hold Biak." Perhaps so, but that did not stop the Allies.

Nashville, once again part of Admiral Berkey's task force and other covering cruisers and destroyers, rendezvoused the morning of May 26 with the attack landing force, known as the Hurricane Attack Force. Nashville proceeded at the unfamiliar and uneasy speed of eight point five knots, matching the slowest towed landing craft and making the ship highly vulnerable to air and submarine attack. It was an uneasy feeling for the crew, to travel so slowly in such a swift and maneuverable ship. The Japanese knew they were coming but had no idea they were coming so soon after Hollandia and Wadke. It was estimated by Allied intelligence that no more than 2,000 Japanese troops held Biak and that it was "not heavily held." It was intelligence in name only. Colonel Naoyuki Kuzume had 10,000 troops under his command including the 222 Regiment, crack veteran troops seasoned in the China campaigns, along with anti-aircraft guns and light tanks. The troops were well-trained and disciplined. And ready to die.

At 0629 May 27, the anniversary of the Japanese Navy, Admiral Fletcher ordered: "Execute landing plan," at which time Nashville, Phoenix, and Boise, old veterans at this, fired 1,000 of their six-inch shells onto buildings, troops, and equipment scattered around the three airfields. Destroyers fired directly onto positions at the landing beaches. Even though, due to planning miscalculations, currents, and smoke-obscured reference points on the island, the troops landed at a different than planned location, they did at least all land at the same location. Albert U. Gaines had two cousins within his field of vision with the landing force, one Marine and one Army, with the Marine about to be seriously wounded in the shoulder.

At 1100 hours four Japanese fighters suddenly appeared over the island and jointly attacked the Nashville scout plane, sending machine gun fire ripping through the fuselage and both the main float and a wing float but somehow missing the crew, then flew away from Nashville at high speed. Late in the day at 1754 hours two Japanese fighter-bombers came in low and fast over the beachhead and dropped three bombs, scoring direct hits on landing ship-tank, LST -456. The screaming planes released the bombs at such a low altitude that they did not explode but rather hit the craft with a sickening metallic thud. Some very astonished, nervous, and lucky sailors quickly picked up the bombs and gingerly tossed them overboard, counting their blessings.

Moments later four twin-engine bombers came roaring in low over the cliffs with two targeting Nashville, and were immediately greeted with intense anti-aircraft fire from Nashville and other ships along with land forces. The massive and accurate onslaught of proximity fuse fire from Nashville and others quickly shot down three of the bombers. The fourth was hit and last seen sputtering away, trailing thick black smoke, and most likely crashed shortly after disappearing from view. Unfortunately one of the three bombers shot down cart-wheeled into the water just past destroyer Sampson and crashed into subchaser SC-699, killing two and wounding eight. It was evident the Japanese were going to come after the Navy this time, unlike Hollandia and Wadke. As the battle for Biak raged on, intelligence discerned heavy naval activity in the area of

Halmahera, Tawi Tawi, and Davao, and the build-up of carrier aircraft within striking distance of Biak. This time intelligence was on the mark. Imperial Headquarters, partly at the urging of Admiral Ugaki who understood the strategic significance of Biak to the defense of the Home Islands, had in fact ordered Admiral Ito's 23rd Air Flotilla to be increased by fifty fighters from Japan and twenty fighters and twenty bombers to be transferred from bases in the Marianas. By May 29 Combined Fleet, caught off guard by the suddenness of the American attack on Biak, hastily drew up plans for its relief, known as Operation Kon. On the thirty-first another twenty bombers, forty-eight fighters, and eight reconnaissance planes were flown into the area. "Kon" entailed moving troops to Biak and an attack on the American ships offshore. Special emphasis was noted for Nashville as a Doolittle raider and occasional MacArthur flagship. Rear Admiral Naomasa Sakonju commanded the naval operations from flagship heavy cruiser Aoba. Admiral Sakonju also had heavy cruisers Myoko and Haguro, battleship Fuso, light cruiser Kinu, and seven destroyers under his command, a formidable naval force in addition to the 23rd Air Flotilla. The Japanese had obviously comprehended the significance of holding onto the three airfields on Biak in the greater scheme of things.

On June 2 the largest Japanese air attack of 1944 to date against Nashville and the Seventh Fleet commenced at 1640 hours with attacks by fifty-four planes against the American beachhead, LSTs, and ships off the coast. Due to weather conditions at Hollandia and Wadke no American planes were present or available. The US Navy was without significant air cover. The relentless air attack went on for sixty-five minutes and was met with massive anti-aircraft fire from both shore locations and Nashville and the ships off the coast. Despite the fact that most of the attack concentrated on the fleet, only one LST-467 had minor damage as a result of a near-miss. The Japanese lost twelve valuable pilots and planes.

Early on June 3 a large Japanese naval force under Admiral Sakonju, including battleship Fuso, multiple destroyers, minelayers, and cruisers was sighted by an American submarine, ruining their plan for a surprise attack against Biak and the American fleet. A Seventh Fleet B24 flying from Wadke sighted the task force and reported back immediately. The operation was cancelled at 2025 against the pleas of the army, and the ships returned to Japanese-held waters. That same day thirty-two Zekes, nine Navy bombers, and ten Army planes of Imperial Japan attacked US Navy destroyers off Bosnik, Biak. One killed and five wounded on destroyer Reid and two wounded on an LCT was the extent of casualties. Eleven Japanese planes were shot down by land, sea, and finally, late-arriving aircraft.

Nashville and her task force under Admiral Berkey had been patrolling the area northeast of Biak guarding against any large enemy naval attacks. Admiral Kinkaid was convinced the Japanese Navy was about to move in great force against his fleet in the waters off Biak so on June 2 he combined both of his cruiser groups, placed them under command of Admiral Crutchley, and ordered them to Humboldt Bay to take on fuel and supplies in anticipation of extended action at sea. The Nashville and other ships of the task force, without carrier air support or the heavy long range guns of battleships, was expected to repulse anything the Japanese Navy threw at them in an effort to retake Biak. And the Japanese had a powerful task force ready to do so.

PBYs had reported enemy ships steaming south towards Biak so Admiral Crutchley was ordered to arrive by 1715 at a point 25 miles north of the eastern coast of Biak and search for Japanese naval forces that may enter the area. Nashville, Phoenix, Australia, Boise, and fourteen destroyers of Task Force 74 and Task Force 75 awaited what would have been a much larger task force of the Japanese Navy. The Nashville task force had been first sighted by a Japanese Army reconnaissance plane and it misidentified many of the ships (a common weakness in the Japanese navy) and reported the force as two carriers, two battleships, and at least ten destroyers. This threw the Japanese into a near panic but that was toned down when, at 2013 hours, a Navy plane reported only four cruisers and eight destroyers.

All other Allied vessels had been informed of Admiral Crutchley's mission and were ordered to stand clear of the cruisers and destroyers and away from the anticipated battle. General Whitehead's bombers at Wakde were placed on alert and the shore batteries on Biak under General Fuller were pointed seaward towards an anticipated Japanese naval attack. Late on June 3rd Japan attacked the Nashville task force with ten Army bombers, nine Navy bombers, and twenty-two Zeros, reporting the sinking of Nashville and one destroyer. It was at least the fifth time Nashville had been reported sunk by the Japanese, all wishful thinking. Nashville had been reported sunk so many times by the Japanese since the Doolittle Raid that even the Japanese no longer believed the reports, with Admiral Sakonju immediately questioning the accuracy. Nashville was not hit at all, but destroyer Reid was slightly damaged.

The Japanese again spotted Task Force 74 and 75 on June 4 while they were still over 100 miles east of Biak and had yet to reach their position point. The Japanese 23rd Air Flotilla ordered twenty-eight fighters and six bombers to attack the ships. It was a clear, beautiful day with the sun slowly descending and not a tropical breeze to be found. As shared by Rufus B. Thompson, Lt. Colonel USMC, stationed in AA control aft, "It was a beautiful, clear day." The ships were just ordered to the standard anti-aircraft maneuvering pattern, at multiple courses, cutting through the calm deep seas at twenty-five knots. At approximately 1735 radar picked up enemy bogeys west and headed towards the ships. At approximately 1740, six Japanese aircraft dove almost straight down and attacked the task force. One in particular had the Nashville in its bombsight as it quickly dove head on at 350 miles per hour, straight at the ship's bow.

Aboard Nashville lookouts were stationed about the ship accordingly but it was radar that first sighted the plane approaching head-on from above. Captain Coney asked Bob Shafer to identify the aircraft. "I was on the bridge at my lookout station and when the radar picked up a plane the captain turned to me and said to identify that aircraft. I got on the phone to 'Foghorn' and said identify that aircraft. 'P-38 he replied.' I turned and told the skipper P-38 and just about that time, wham, we got hit." Foghorn could not have been more mistaken.

Fortunately, the lookout at the point of the bow, an African-American cook, who was in a prone position looking up into the sun since that is where planes liked to attack from, not the regulation position nor field of view for lookouts, spotted the plane and yelled, "My God, there is one right above us!" then immediately fired which caused the pilot to suddenly veer left to avoid being hit just as he released his 100kg bomb. That cook, likely relaxing a little more than he should have, may have saved the ship from a devastating and deadly direct hit. As it was, the bomb plunged into the water just ten feet starboard. Albert Landi saw "one coming in and began machine gunning over the bridge as I reached same, proceeding to my battle station. His fire was off a little and was shooting over our heads, and then he headed towards our fantail and dropped a 500 pound skip bomb."

Joe Fales was strapped into the gun director, heard machine gun fire, and then saw a plane that seemed right on top of him. "There came this plane, I could see the pilot, I can see him today just as plain as I could see him then, with his leather helmet and his goggles and white scarf, typical Japanese pilot." Just then an officer relieved him and Joe bolted out of the tub and started down the ladder that went to the boat deck and he went down that ladder with uncharacteristic ease. "I sailed down it because the bomb had hit and raised the Nashville up, but when it went down I found myself right back at the top of the ladder again." Joe made it to his battle station as sight setter in an aft turret unscathed.

James Clark distinctly remembers the incident. "I was a first loader on one of the 40mm guns. The gun crew was trying to line up on a plane coming in at about 3 o'clock and the director crew was trying to line up on a plane coming in at about 12 o'clock. Since the director and gun must be within a few degrees before the director crew can aim and shoot, nothing was happening. I was standing there with a clip of ammo in my hands waiting for the plane to start shooting, knowing it would be the end for the crew. The next thing was the bomb falling from the plane looking like it was going to hit me in the nose, but as it came closer it curved away and passed so close I could almost reach and touch it."

Joseph A. Graves SM2c was receiving a light signal from the destroyer astern and starboard when he heard the Jap plane coming. "I turned and saw the rising sun on it and yelled for my recorder to hit the deck. We didn't even have a helmet on. It was too close for comfort."

The term near-miss is misleading. While the bomb itself may be a "near-hit," its impact is anything but as the concussion does more than a minimum of damage with shock waves alone. The explosion five feet below the surface sent a column of water shooting forty feet into the air and shook the ship throughout, vibrated it both horizontally and vertically, and immediately putting both gyros out of commission. The ship took damage below the waterline with the hull penetrated in six places, affecting five fuel oil tanks and 38,000 gallons of fuel. Bomb fragments tore jagged holes in the side, rivets sheared off, and the shell plating rolled up and outward in one place and was crushed inward in another, doors and hatches bent, and the third deck was buckled up. At a speed of twenty-five knots sea water was forced into the forward starboard side of Nashville like a collapsed dam, flooding no less than ten compartments in addition to the fuel tanks. Nashville quickly listed three degrees to starboard; the bow raised over two feet while the stern settled over three feet deeper into the 1,200 fathom depths.

James Clark said, "There was the explosion, the ship shuddered, and I'm thinking here we go swimming. Then Tatum (part of gun crew) yelled to Papa Tague (gun crew) 'break out the dress blues we're going to Uncle Sugar Able.' That brought me back out of the shock of the moment and every one else on the gun crew." Even down in the fire room John W. Bosier CMM and the others "felt the ship shudder."

George L. Bustin GM2c was on duty in gun director two and felt the water spray hit him and smelled the explosive chemicals of the bomb despite his height off the main deck "I heard the blast and felt the water from the explosion even at the height of my station."One hundred and seventy-five crew's lockers and 169 bunks were severely damaged. Bob Shafer remembers, "The irony was that this was where all the lookouts slept, including Herb Taylor who escaped being wounded despite the fact he was laying on his bunk at the time, so they had only the clothes on their backs, had to sleep topside in life jacket containers or any other shelter they could find, taking handouts of clothing wherever they could get them. We slept wherever we could; you had to fend for yourself. I slept in a lifejacket compartment for two weeks. And we lost all our clothes and Supply had none to issue so people donated their cast-off uniforms. For the next three months when the lookouts were not on watch they went to school, checking and identifying all aircraft of the Japanese air forces." No lookout ever misidentified a Japanese plane as an American plane for the remainder of the war.

Nearly forty years after the war, lookout Herb Taylor was visiting the famous International Experimental Aircraft Association's annual fly-in at Oshkosh, Wisconsin and he was frustrated by his inability to visually identify and remember the multitude of WWII aircraft all about him. But as soon as they took to the air, Herb could easily identify each one by the sound of their engines.

The sister ship of Nashville, USS Phoenix was also hit by a near-miss with shrapnel killing one sailor and damage to various compartments, but less extensive than Nashville's.

Despite taking on tons of water, losing some speed and maneuverability, and listing in the water, Nashville did not quit, did not hesitate, and did not deviate from her duty. She kept her position in the task force and continued to fight off heavy air attacks. While she kept pace with the rest of the task force, brave men had a brave task to perform. Chief Shipfitter William Smith and others had to go below the waterline and quickly shore up the bulging bulkheads. "We were scared but we knew we had to do it. We estimated later that there was 500 tons of water on the other side of us." That water could have burst through the weakened bulkhead at any moment, crushing and drowning Smith and his crewmates, but if they did not do their job the ship itself was in immediate jeopardy. They did their job and did it well, working under extreme pressure in a noisy and chaotic environment, with the ship maneuvering against submarines and air attacks. Ed Yusko stated, "We had very good damage control. They shored up the bulkheads quickly. If it wasn't for them all that water would have completely crushed the bulkheads and it would have been a whole different story."

The combined task force of cruisers and destroyers, with Nashville and Phoenix damaged, finally reached assigned position at 1900 hours. The ships patrolled the areas west and south of the island as it was expected that any Japanese landing would most likely be attempted at Wardo on the west coast of Biak. Nothing was found in the way of the enemy so the combined task force then returned to its original patrol position northeast of Biak to intercept any incoming invasion fleet. As they were passing through the channel at Owi-Biak at 0225 June 5, four Japanese torpedo planes dropped down for a low, wave skimming head on attack, releasing at least three torpedoes that failed to find their marks to the great relief of the sailors and marines onboard. Later still, early on June 5 Japanese bombers attacked Wadke Island and inflicted heavy damage on the 100 plus parked planes caught on the airfield. The anticipated invasion had not occurred but many still expected it to come, and soon. But for now Nashville and other ships could safely anchor in the shallow Biak harbor where the crew could dive off the ship into the clear blue water. George L. Bustin GM2c was one such crewman and quite a strong swimmer. He gracefully dove off the bow of the ship and plunged deep enough to hit his head on the bottom. "Always the water was so clear in the Pacific that it looked like it was only five feet deep when it was really thirty or so, but this time it was really shallow."

Nashville was then ordered to Seeadler Harbor, Manus for repairs but her bomb damage was so extensive she was re-ordered to Espiritu Santo, New Herbrides on June 14, escorted by destroyers Warrington and Balch. Nashville arrived on June 18 and immediately entered dry dock where a navy repair ship AR-12 tied up alongside and got to work around the clock repairing Nashville. Shipfitters, electricians, metalsmiths, radio technicians, and the like diligently worked to send Nashville back to the battle zone where she was needed as quickly as possible, in fact quicker as America's repair crews did phenomenally for so many ships during the war. One of the interesting things the repair crew did was to fill part of her outer bulkheads with cement as a structural reinforcement. Astonished sailors questioned the logic of inserting such a heavy substance into a ship but were assured it would work perfectly well, and it did.

On July 13, 1944 the fully repaired Nashville, escorted by destroyers Loeser and Greenwood, departed Espiritu Santo and sailed for Sydney where they anchored from July 17-25 with the crew enjoying one of their favorite liberty ports, certainly the favorite once they sailed past Honolulu. But liberty comes to an end and Nashville arrived in Milne Bay, New Guinea on July 29 to resume her wartime duties. August was a routine month of patrols in the New Guinea area. Routine usually involving air attacks, some bombardment, submarine evasions, and the like. The stress was constant, ebbing and flowing with the circumstances. Stress can take its toll on men in many ways but rarely overtly and detrimentally on the ship. One such case was the sailor that just decided one morning he was going to jump overboard and swim to the nearest island, just off the stern, at least in his reality. Trouble was the ship was nowhere even close to being within site of land and the sailor jumped and kept swimming. Lucky for him, there were no serious operations going on at the moment so a launch was sent to retrieve him before he could drown. He was transferred to the hospital at the next stop.

***

Morotai
(September-November 44)

Due to the shortage of landing craft as a result of the Normandy invasion in Europe, the staffs of Admiral Nimitz and General MacArthur revised their overall plans and decided on somewhat of an intermediate step on the road to the liberation of the Philippines. Morotai was chosen as that step. Whether this was considered as the final stage of the greater New Guinea campaign or the introductory stage of the coming Philippine campaign due to geography was nothing more than the academic half-empty half-full argument and as about as useless. There was no argument that Morotai would be another step closer to General MacArthur's personal goal of returning to the Philippines and keeping his word and (and by virtue of his position) that of the United States to return.

Morotai was chosen partially due to the fact that the Japanese had 37,000 troops and nine airfields on the other likely stepping stone, Halmahera Island, with its natural defenses favoring the enemy. Morotai, a thick jungle of mountains, was forty-five miles long and twenty-five miles wide. It was believed that no more than 500 enemy troops were on the island but many thousands more were available as reinforcements on neighboring islands. There was but one unfinished airfield of military value, located on a coastal plain on the southern part of the island.

Admiral Berkey commanded the assault naval support group consisting of Nashville with General MacArthur aboard and two other light cruisers, two Australian heavy cruisers, eight American, and two Australian destroyers. On September 13 this task force, along with the escort carrier group consisting of six CVEs, and the transports carrying 16,482 troops, rendezvoused off Vogelkop and sailed to the coast of Morotai completely undetected by the Japanese.

September 15 was D-Day, a fair and pleasant enough day with but minor partial overcast to diffuse the tropical sun. At 0510 Nashville and the other ships under Admiral Berkey's command maneuvered into position to do what they had done so well so many times prior, bombard the enemy with deadly and accurate six-inch shelling at a steady and absurdly quick pace. It was somewhat of a diversion with Nashville shelling an airfield and installations at Kaoe Bay on Halmahara Island

and the invasion fleet landing at Morotai. The shelling lasted for nearly an hour and not a single shot was returned by the enemy.

Once the firing ceased Nashville and the other cruisers quickly steamed across the Strait to Cape Gila so that Admiral Barbey and General Hall could board Nashville to meet with General MacArthur. The General and staff spent three hours ashore looking over the situation. After Admiral Barbey and General Hall debarked Nashville, she and the remainder of Admiral Berkey's group took patrol position south of Morotai awaiting an enemy naval attack or a call for further fire support on the island. Neither occurred. The landings were unopposed. By the sixteenth, Liberty ships were arriving with supplies for building a large supply and air base. Half of the Japanese had been eliminated and about 200 took to the hills where they were left to their own fate. The assault and capture of Morotai coincided with the same on bloody Pelelieu, finally bringing together the tenacious American campaigns of the Central Pacific and Southwest Pacific Forces. Morotai became a very useful base in terms of launching light and medium bombers and short range fighters into Leyte, Philippines and staging for the Leyte campaign. The US now had control of the eastern approaches to Leyte Gulf and Leyte was the door to the liberation of the Philippines.

As October 1944 arrived the various naval and army forces under General MacArthur began to build up at multiple points along coastal New Guinea and at Manus as MacArthur and his staff once again used Nashville as an invasion flagship. MacArthur flew from Brisbane to Hollandia and boarded the ship. This time, Billy Rae Lyerly, who had been aboard Nashville since June 1941, was assigned to MacArthur and wrote up the convoy orders for the much-heralded return to the Philippines. The Third Fleet had a powerful contingent of eighteen fleet size carriers, six battleships, seventeen cruisers, and sixty-four destroyers. The Seventh Fleet comprised over 700 ships including 157 combatants. Combined with the ground forces accumulating daily it was an awesome and inspiring show of force and a spectacular testament to both the industrial workers of the United States and the military, from almost a standing start with a severely limited number of ships and troops on December 7, 1941 when the Japanese extended their cannot refuse invitation to join the war. It was absolutely the most powerful fleet ever assembled in history (surpassing in terms of firepower that of the Normandy invasion) and would become more so in the coming months and battles in the Pacific.

On October 16 Nashville sailed from Hollandia and on the twentieth she steamed in convoy into Leyte Gulf. MacArthur noted in his diary, "The stygian waters below and the black sky above seemed to conspire in wrapping us in an invisible cloak, as we lay to and waited for dawn before entering Leyte Gulf." On October 24 with General MacArthur still embarked, Nashville, providing air cover, joined twenty-nine Liberty ships and three amphibious force flagships in San Pedro Bay, anchored off Tacloban. Nashville, glistening with stars and brass on its bridge, was to bring victory as she had before. That night GM2c George Bustin and others on watch saw light flashes forty miles on the distant southern horizon as the Battle of Surigao Strait raged on. If not for the fact that the General was on board, Nashville would have been in the thick of that battle as were the other combatant ships she had traveled with into San Pedro Bay. Among these ships with Nashville were six of the pre-war navy battleships, five of which had been severely damaged or sunk at Pearl Harbor, only to rise from the muddy bottom of Pearl Harbor and fight again. As they took the brunt of the first day of the war, they were directly affecting the last great naval battle and the hastening of the end of the Japanese Empire.

During the afternoon of October 24, Vice Admiral Thomas Kinkaid, Commander Seventh Fleet, met with MacArthur. It is generally believed the Admiral requested the General to leave the Nashville as she was badly needed in the upcoming battle. MacArthur understood the risks but stated he wanted to remain on board, that he welcomed to be a witness to what many thought could be the last great surface naval battle not only of the war but perhaps in history. Admiral Kinkaid would not take responsibility for sending the General into harm's way. While MacArthur understood he requested that he would like to join the Admiral at his station on the Wasatch ACG-9 but of course this was rejected by the Admiral with the same logic. MacArthur remained on the Nashville that night, effectively keeping her off the battle line. What might have happened if MacArthur had debarked when requested? What new challenge had Nashville missed?

Early the next morning Kinkaid sent a message to McArthur requesting he immediately leave the Nashville, as the ship was urgently needed with her experienced crew and full load of fuel and armor-piercing ammunition. A large portion of the Japanese fleet had already passed through the San Bernardino Straits and was attacking the essentially unarmored jeep carriers and a few destroyers and destroyer escorts east of Leyte. MacArthur and staff debarked in a flash and Nashville was off and running once again at flank speed towards a superior Japanese naval force, something she had done throughout the war without hesitation or doubt. But by the time Nashville arrived on scene in full battle stations the Japanese had broken off the attack and retreated.

The first recorded planned kamikaze attack of the war took place on October 25, 1944 off Samar Island, Philippines with two escort carriers damaged and one sunk. The men of Nashville no doubt heard about it and had their individual and collective thoughts, but it did not register deeply, what with their own duties and dangers and experience with reports, both official and not. Later, it would become the most memorable part of their wartime experience.

On October 29, Admiral Kinkaid reorganized Seventh Fleet, transferring many ships to Ulithi. Remaining as part of the Seventh Fleet to protect Leyte Gulf from Japanese naval forces was Nashville along with battleships California, Pennsylvania, Mississippi, cruisers Phoenix, Boise, and (HMAS) Shropshire, along with thirteen destroyers.

By November 1 the situation at Leyte was not in the least bit rosy for the Allied forces. Japanese naval forces were reportedly ready to make a major attack in the area and as an illustration of the tentativeness of the foothold in the Philippines, the Japanese had regained control of the skies as there simply were not enough Navy, Marine, and Army aircraft yet available in the forward area. The American Navy was reduced in strength, the jeep carriers were long gone to Manus for repairs and their airpower was missed. Battleships California, Pennsylvania, and Mississippi, Aussie heavy cruiser Shropshire, light cruisers Nashville, Phoenix, and Boise, and a dozen destroyers were it for the Allies. They were in fact the entire Allied Navy in the area. The Japanese were staging reinforcement planes into airfields in Leyte and troops in Ormoc Bay on the western coast. A major confrontation was brewing with neither side willing or able to lose a decisive battle that would no doubt drive the calendar of events for the remainder of the war.

At 0950 on November 1, Japanese planes pushed past the fleet's brave but meager combat air patrol and attacked ships in Leyte Gulf. Several cruisers and destroyers were damaged and one destroyer sunk in the attacks through the day. Some were bombed but there were direct kamikaze attacks, still quite a new weapon in the Japanese arsenal. The kamikazes were a bad dream that would later develop into a nightmare. During the period November 16-29, kamikazes struck attack transports Alpine and James O'Hara, light cruisers St. Louis and Montpelier, battleships Colorado and Maryland, and destroyers Saufley and Aulick.

Throughout this time, as Nashville served as General MacArthur's flagship, she did patrol and support duty. Having the General on board always brought a certain amount of interest from the press and decorum from the crew. Some men were interested in the general while others had little or no interest. The General and his staff were treated obviously with the utmost respect as was appropriate for his position. One evening the General was having problems with his commode in the Head in the Admiral's Cabin, his cabin whenever he stayed on board. Chief Shipfitter William "Bill" Smith was ordered personally to take care of the general by Warrant Carpenter Cramer. "So I went up to the Shipfitter's shop, got some tools and a new flushmeter valve, and headed for the Admiral's Cabin. There was a sentry outside the door so I told him my mission. He said 'go ahead, he's expecting you.' I opened the door and saw the General sitting at a big table with a bunch of maps in front of him. He looked up and I said, 'Good evening General,' and saluted. He saluted back and said, 'Good evening.' I said, 'I'm Chief Shipfitter Smith,' and to this day I don't know if I said 'I understand there is something wrong in your head' or 'the' Head. It seemed to me he hesitated a moment and then said, 'Oh yes, go right ahead.' I went in and it was the flushometer, full of barnacles. I cleaned it, put it back, flushed it two or three times and told him it was OK if he would like to check it. He said, 'No, if it suits you it suits me. Thank you very much. Goodnight.' Well, I said goodnight and as I walked down the deck I began to wonder what I had said, and I will never know but I hope I said, 'I understand there's something wrong with the Head.'"

James D. Baccus saw him one day "sitting in the doorway of the Admiral's Cabin and several of us asked him to give us his autograph, which he did. Baccus of 1st Division remembers talking with the General.

"He borrowed my pen, signed it, and handed me the note but did not give me the pen back. He asked what else I wanted and I told him my pen. He grunted and returned it."

MacArthur liked to go ashore and get a feel for what was happening on the ground, a logical practice for a career Army general. Sailors like to go ashore too, especially if they are not permitted to do so. While Nashville was anchored off an island off-limits to enlisted men, Charles E. Purdue and some other adventuresome sailors decided to assume responsibility for one of the ship's Launches and visit the island. It remains a mystery how they were able to take the Launch, but they did so and docked it at a pier on the island. No sooner had they jumped out of the boat and started eagerly down the dock, they ran directly into General MacArthur and Admiral Halsey. Fearing the worst, the men received but a piercing cold stare from Halsey and a terse "Carry on men." Lucky they were.

Biak "near-hit" damage that nearly sank the ship, June 1944

Nashville in floating drydock for Biak damage repairs, June 28, 1944

Nashville's Biak near-miss as seen from USS Mississippi BB41

CHAPTER 8
Kamikaze: Hell on Deck

***

"Too much cannot be said for the initiative and bravery of these men. They walked right into the fire without a moment's hesitation."
-Captain Charles E. Coney of Roanoke, VA, Commander of USS Nashville.

"We had thought we could easily tackle them and that a race steeped in material comfort, seemingly absorbed in a hunt for pleasure, was spiritually degenerate. It was too late when we discovered the Americans, the true Americans. They stood up for the defense of liberty, and once they stood up for that great idea, no price was too dear for them."
-Masataka Chihaya, Officer, Imperial Japanese Navy

***

The major step in the United States and General MacArthur fulfilling the promise of returning to liberate the Philippine people began in early October 1944 as over 700 ships of the 7th and 3rd fleets gathered near New Guinea, the most powerful naval force the world have ever seen at that time (more powerful fleets would inevitably be used in the invasions of Iwo Jim and Okinawa and certainly in the planned invasion of Japan). The American 7th Fleet alone was more powerful than any other country's entire navy, including the Japanese. In fact, Admiral Halsey would later write, "Our naval power in the western Pacific was such that we could have challenged the combined fleets of the world." October 20, 1944 was designated as 'A Day' by General MacArthur (to distinguish it from 'D Day' at Normandy) and sailors and Marines alike were getting antsy to get moving. On October 10th ships pulled anchor and headed for the entrance of Leyte Gulf known as Point Fin (L10 d 28'30"N, long 125 d 56'20"E) ever alert for submarine and air attacks, but fortunately they never materialized as neither did reported Japanese surface forces lurking near the Celebes. The weather was clear, hot, and humid, and men were either on watch or resting as much as possible with thoughts on the coming action. Tokyo Rose was busy with her propaganda lies and knew General MacArthur was aboard the Nashville as his flagship, marking the ship as a prime target for the Japanese again.

The crew of the Nashville had been through a great deal during the war and had survived, frequently defying overwhelming odds. From the North Atlantic to the Aleutians to 600 miles off the coast of Japan to Wake to Midway and more, they had come through whenever and however needed. While they had their share of inevitable accidents both on board, most notably the turret explosion, and in port, and had experienced a harrowing near miss that opened up the port side, they had escaped without casualties as a result of enemy action. It was beginning to look as if perhaps they would get through this war personally unscathed. America was winning, the Japanese tsunami of military victories and criminal occupation was being reversed, and while everyone knew life in a war was tentative and fragile at best and the war was far from over, it was evident that it was only a matter of time before complete victory was achieved. It was not a situation of feeling lucky but more of one that there was hope and one could begin to think about the future, something many of the crew felt they could not realistically do until now even though they talked of it frequently, especially the variety of "what are you going to do when the war is over?" that dealt more with dreams and diversion from the daily stress than of a sense of reality for a foreseeable future. Men like Albert Gaines, married just seven months prior to volunteering for service "thought a lot about how life would be back home after the war." As did all others.

Japan was losing the war and while the reasons were numerous and at times complicated and culturally driven, they were also irreversible, and attempts to rectify the situation by the Japanese were deadly and wasteful to both sides and an inevitable failure. The Japanese generals and admirals knew their situation was on the verge of becoming desperate. The dream of the Greater East Asia Co-Prosperity Sphere, political nomenclature for Japanese hegemony and empire over all of Asia and most of the Pacific in order to feed the Japanese war machine and home islands, was being replaced by a vision of forcing the Americans into a position to be defeated in a singular great sea battle in order for Japan to sue for peace and hold onto the few pacific possessions she still had control of, as well as to forestall major damage to the home islands. In a sense, it was to get a global time-out on the war until the Japanese military and emperor, who contrary to popular belief was not only aware of Japanese atrocities in China and throughout the conquered territories but was actively involved in discussions and planning of military campaigns, until such time as the militarists could once again unleash a powerful fury of violence on the world.

In Japan, away from the deprivations and defeats of the Pacific war, Operation Sho-Go (Victory Operation) planning was completed in late July 1944. Developed after the Americans penetrated the Japanese defenses at the Marianas and New Guinea, Operation Sho was to commit all resources to a final victorious and decisive battle (*kantai kessen*) wherever the US struck again in force. The Japanese Supreme War Council submitted the four part plan to the emperor. Plan 1, believed to be the most likely event, was designed to counter an American attack and invasion of the Philippines, the area of attack championed successfully by MacArthur. Plan 2 was to counter an American attack on Formosa, the area of attack favored by Admiral Nimitz and the Navy. Plan 3 was to counter an attack on the Japanese home islands of Honshu and Kyushu, and Plan 4 Hokkaido and the northern territories. The intransient Japanese remained fatally loyal to the flawed strategy that gave birth to the attack on Pearl Harbor, still seeking to annihilate the increasingly powerful US Navy in a single war ending sea battle. The Nashville, as General MacArthur's flagship and an integral part of the invasion of the Philippines, in effect triggered the execution of Operation Sho-Go Plan 1 at 1701 on October 18, 1944 with the pre-invasion action at Leyte. Admiral Toyoda was alerted by search radar on the four tiny islands (Dinagat, Calicoan, Suluan, and Homonohon) at the extreme reaches of the two entrances to Leyte Gulf, of the approaching invasion fleet at 0749 on October 17 and formally issued the "Execute Sho-Go" at 1410. For the Japanese, the decisive battle area was thus chosen and operations began.

Sho-Go Plan 1 was massive in scale as well as hope, involving land-based aircraft, four separate fleets spread out across the Pacific, decoy carrier forces, the two largest warships in the world, the Yamato and

Mushahi, and the flawed Japanese naval mindset of engaging the enemy fleet in a trap to annihilate them and end the war in a single victory. It was doomed to failure in hindsight.

Vice Admiral Takijiro Ohnishi flew direct from Tokyo to Manila on October 17 to assume command of the First Air Fleet, and quickly and uncharacteristically visited troops in the field at Mabalacat to discuss a monumental and urgent matter. Mabalacat was a remote Philippine village that served as the headquarters of the 201st Air Group. The Admiral brought news from Imperial General Headquarters that illustrated the desperate Japanese situation in the war as well as the militaristic and monolithic nature of Japan's developed self-identity. More importantly, it was news that would have a dramatic impact on the Nashville and her crew to a greater extent than any other event of the war.

Vice Admiral Ohnishi's mission was to provide air cover for Vice Admiral Kurita's Second Fleet in their attempt to penetrate the carriers, battleships, and cruisers of the invasion fleet and destroy the invasion forces. The Second Fleet was the majority of the Japanese naval forces concentrated in the Pacific. But US Navy airpower had been extensively effective in destroying Japanese air forces in preparation for the invasion. Ohnishi brought a plan to maximize use of the remaining Japanese aircraft in the vicinity to smash the US Navy to the extent they were no longer a major threat to the Second Fleet. The plan was to organize suicide units of aircraft armed with 250 kilogram or larger bombs to crash into ships, especially aircraft carriers which were not only laden with planes to threaten the Second Fleet but also bombs, fuel and unprotected flight decks that made them deadly vulnerable to aircraft. If Ohnishi could sink or disable the carriers the massive Second Fleet could cut its way through the invasion force and hand the Americans a massive defeat and save the empire.

On October 20, 1944 the 201st Air Group, battle-tested veterans all, formed the Shimpu Attack Unit (Shimpu means kamikaze or "Divine Wind") composed of four subunits named Yamazakura (Wild Cherry Blossom), Yamato (Ancient Japan), Asahi (Rising Sun) and Shikishima (area of Japan), composed of twenty-four men and led by twenty-three-year-old naval academy graduate Lieutenant Yukio Seki, at Mabalacat air field. The names were symbolically taken from the poem "Waka" by Norinaga Motoori, a nationalist scholar of the Tokugawa Period. This very same day Nashville was off Leyte as General MacArthur's flagship for the invasion of the Philippines. Nashville was also Admiral Kinkaid's flagship of the assault force consisting of over 130 ships and auxiliary craft along with twenty-three torpedo boats and 30,000 troops.

Kamikaze planes approached a target from either a very high or very low altitude with each having advantages and disadvantages. A high altitude approaching 17,000-20,000 feet made the plane near impossible to sight from sea level and it took interceptor planes some time to reach that level. A lower level approach near sea level negated the American advantage of radar and was difficult for visual interception as well. This approach entails hugging the sea level and then, when a target was discerned, the plane climbed quickly to 1,000-1,200 feet and then dove steeply into the target. Both tactics were effective with the low level approach being particularly appropriate when launching land-based kamikazes at ships close to the land mass.

General MacArthur, impressed by the officers and men of the Nashville, had once again selected her as his flagship and this time for the most important and personally moving task of the war, his triumphant return to the Philippines. The Nashville, fresh from the Hollandia and Biak bombardments of New Guinea, had left Hollandia on October 16 and brought the General 1,250 miles and sailed into Leyte Gulf on a moonless night, giving him a ringside seat of the bombardment and invasion which MacArthur witnessed from the ship's bridge the next morning before retiring to his cabin for an early lunch.

MacArthur had long fought for an invasion of the Philippines as opposed to the Navy preference of a more direct attack against Formosa, severing more supply lines and communications lines with fuel sources in Borneo and Sumatra. Besides the fact MacArthur felt he had given his word with his comment "I shall return," he also believed it was politically the right thing to do. And there was the matter of the remaining American survivors of the Bataan Death March to liberate. MacArthur, with the help of Admiral "Bull" Halsey, convinced the Joint Chiefs of Staff that the Philippines were the right target.

The Japanese were well alerted as American intelligence picked up over a dozen secret dispatches by the Japanese relating to the disposition of the invasion forces and the subsequent marshalling of imperial navy forces from as far away as the Japanese Inland Sea and Singapore. As it was, waves of American troops were landing on Leyte by 1000 hours on October 20.

MacArthur was on the bridge with Captain C.E. Coney early that morning as Nashville knifed through dark waters towards Leyte, dodging floating mines amidst the sighting of an enemy submarine periscope and the resultant destroyer depth charging. Richard Metcalf looked at MacArthur and thought, "his uniform was so starched that I pictured it standing up by itself when he removed it on retiring." The ship reached its designated spot two miles offshore and dropped anchor. After an early lunch in his cabin MacArthur boarded his landing barge at 1247 hours, dressed in freshly pressed khakis, braided hat, and his famous sunglasses, standing behind Philippines President Osmena, Resident Commissioner Romulo, Chief of Staff Sutherland, and Air Commander Kenney.

MacArthur's landing craft got stuck on a sandbar or reef just about ten yards short of the beach and the party had to wade ashore. The resultant photograph is world famous and the object of more than a little derision and suspicion, including comments regarding staging and re-shooting the event for posterity (and the General's career). But William J. Dunn, the media representative for CBS Radio, who was on the barge as part of the media team says "it was all the real thing."

No matter how he traversed the last ten yards, the Nashville had delivered MacArthur back to the Philippines. The event of the day was to be a speech to the Philippine people, and to the world that MacArthur had returned. A radio transmitter mounted on a weapons carrier was brought up. The transmitter was directly linked to a much more powerful master transmitter aboard Nashville. Speaking deliberately and clearly into a microphone, MacArthur noted:

"People of the Philippines: I have returned. By the grace of Almighty God our forces stand again on Philippine soil—soil consecrated in the blood of our two peoples. We have come, dedicated and committed to the task of destroying every vestige of enemy control over your daily lives, and of restoring upon a foundation of indestructible strength, the liberties of your people. At my side is your president, Sergio Osmena, a worthy successor of that great patriot, Manuel Quezon, with members of his cabinet. The seat of your government is now, therefore, firmly re-established on Philippine soil.
The hour of your redemption is here. Your patriots have demonstrated

an unswerving and resolute devotion to the principles of freedom that challenge the best that is written on the pages of human history. I now call upon your supreme effort that the enemy may know, from the temper of an aroused people within, that he has a force there to contend with no less violent than is the force committed from without. Rally to me. Let the indomitable spirit of Bataan and Corregidor lead on. As the lines of battle roll forward to bring you within the zones of operation, rise and strike. Strike at every favorable opportunity. For your homes and hearths, strike! For future generations of your sons and daughters, strike! In the name of your sacred dead, strike! Let no heart be faint. Let every arm be steeled. The guidance of Divine God points the way. Follow in His name to the Holy Grail of righteous victory."

It was a day for speechmaking. President Roosevelt made his own historic speech.

"The suffering, humiliation and mental torture that you have endured since the barbarous, unprovoked and treacherous attack upon the Philippines nearly three long years ago have aroused in the hearts of the American people a righteous anger, a stern determination to punish the guilty and a fixed resolve to restore peace and order and decency to an enraged world.
On this occasion of the return of General MacArthur to Philippine soil with our airmen, our soldiers and our sailors, we renew our pledge. We and our Philippine brothers in arms—-with the help of Almighty God—-will drive out the invader; we will destroy his power to wage war again, and we will restore a world of dignity and freedom—-a world of confidence and honesty and peace."

At 1300 Nashville got underway and then sounded general quarters one minute later due to unidentified aircraft sighted in the vicinity. At 1352 she anchored in San Pedro Bay, Leyte, off Red Beach. After a brief note to President Roosevelt written on a writing tablet under a palm tree and a cursory inspection of front line troops, MacArthur returned to the Nashville at 1600 and the familiarity of his cabin before night fell upon the battlefields of Leyte. A minute after the General embarked, Japanese torpedo planes were reported approaching from the north and once again general quarters was sounded and the ship got underway at

1619. Moments later the USS Honolulu was torpedoed off the southern invasion beach. Over 150 Japanese air attacks were flown against the Leyte fleet.

It was evident by October 23 that Admiral Toyoda was going to commit the entire Japanese fleet to the battle for Leyte and Nashville was needed by Admiral Kinkaid for the coming battle of Surigao Strait, part of the greater Battle of Leyte, the greatest naval battle of all time. Kinkaid in fact requested that MacArthur move his headquarters and staff ashore specifically so that Nashville could join the battle line. At first MacArthur wanted to remain onboard but Kinkaid said he could not commit Nashville to battle as long as MacArthur was onboard so the General relented and moved his staff ashore to safer quarters on October 24.

Nashville would see plenty of action, fighting ninety relentless air attacks over forty days. Over seventy Japanese airfields of various size and capacity were within striking distance of Nashville and the invasion fleet. On the night of October 26th at 1954 hours Nashville, as part of Task Force 77 picked up an enemy plane on radar sixteen miles off the starboard bow. Gun and damage control crews along with everyone on board were ready and waited nearly a minute for the plane to come into reasonable gun range before opening fire with four of her five-inch and sixteen of her 20mm guns. At 4,000 yards the plane was but 150 feet above the dark water, traveling at 150 knots. Obviously this was a "Kate" or a "Jill" on a torpedo run. The Japanese plane flew close past the starboard side of a screening destroyer and then banked hard starboard aiming for the Nashville amidships. At 700 yards the plane released a deadly torpedo at Nashville. If the torpedo had traveled just one knot faster, if the Nashville had traveled at just one know slower, if the plane had banked one degree harder, the Nashville would have suffered a devastating torpedo hit on her starboard stern. As it was, the tons of high explosive passed less than fifteen yards off Nashville's stern. She had survived yet another close call.

Morning, afternoon, and at times each night, Nashville and others continually fought off determined Japanese air attacks over the next few days during which time four destroyers were damaged and one sunk. USS Abner Read DD-526 was hit by a kamikaze plane, quickly engulfed in flames and secondary explosions, and just before she sank she jettisoned her torpedoes causing Nashville and others ships to hard maneuver to avoid being struck.

Interestingly, after the war "Eye of the Tiger" General Yamashita stated he did not believe MacArthur set his HQ up on Leyte so early or that he was on board the Nashville, so close and so potentially vulnerable to massive suicide attacks. He thought the MacArthur landing photographs were fakes and said if he had known the facts he would have massed an all-out (air) attack on the Nashville or MacArthur's headquarters ashore to kill him in revenge for the attack and death of Admiral Yamamoto.

As it was, Nashville continued to be target enough, fighting off constant Japanese air attacks. Lieutenant Gerald T. Smith was the popular Nashville chaplain and was an eyewitness to many such attacks. "We were off Leyte on December 11 when destroyer Reid was attacked by Japanese planes and blew up and sank in less than two minutes, after taking three direct hits in succession. I had often conducted church services aboard this fighting little destroyer. That day off Leyte, about a dozen Jap planes suddenly appeared and attacked the Reid. The Reid's crew was expecting such an attack and began firing as soon as the Jap planes were within range. But the Japs scored three hits: Bang! Bang! Bang! And in less time than it takes to tell it, the Reid blew up and sank. I didn't see how any of her crew could have come through alive, but we (Nashville) picked up 150 of them and only twenty-eight of those were injured."

On December 12, 1944 USS Nashville left berth #32 in San Pedro Bay off Leyte Island, Philippines as part of Task Group 78.3, also known as the Visayan Attack Force on orders of Rear Admiral A.D. Struble, en route to the vicinity of Mindoro Island, Philippines for purposes of bombarding enemy installations and forces as support for the landing of American troops, steaming high speed at night to avoid kamikazes. The task force was divided into three groups of which Admiral Strubble took direct command of one, the Mindoro Attack Group led by Nashville, twelve escorting destroyers, eight destroyer transports, thirty LSTs, twelve LSMs, thirty-one LCIs, ten large minesweepers, seven small minesweepers, and fourteen miscellaneous smaller craft. Nashville was chosen to lead the operation and had all the brass aboard to prove it. Rear Admiral Arthur D. Struble, Navy Commander of the Mindoro Operation, his staff, and Brigadier General William C. Dunkel, handpicked by MacArthur, and his staff, were aboard the Nashville. Operating in the

Sulu Sea in support was a group of battleships, escort carriers, cruisers, and destroyers. Anticipating air battles, the fighter plane complement of sixteen per escort carrier was increased to twenty-four, reducing the torpedo bomber strength from twelve to nine.

Mindoro was needed to build airfields so that Allied forces could attack Japanese air forces operating from Luzon and to provide air cover for the planned January invasion at Lingayen and the liberation of Luzon itself. The Navy's spearhead into the Mindoro area was a calculated risk and nothing less than a mission of the highest danger to ships and men. The task force would pass several enemy held islands and be nearly surrounded by twelve or more active Japanese airfields on Luzon and surrounding islands, upon arrival near San Jose. Additionally, the ships would be 262 miles from the nearest American airfield at Dulag, when the normal operational range of American land-based fighters was 260 miles at the time, giving new meaning to the term pushing the envelope.

While Japanese resistance on Mindoro was not expected to be heavy nor prolonged due to the relatively light number of troops on the island, air resistance was expected to be fierce, specifically from land-based kamikazes. A split-responsibility air plan was worked out with the Navy and Army, dividing duties by time of day, area, and eventually dates. The V Army Air Force would provide some additional help to the Navy Combat Air Patrols in the Mindanao Sea during passage and provide total coverage after dusk through N-Day (Mindoro D-Day) on December 15, after which time they would provide support duties at the landing site. A further decision was made that Admiral Halsey's Third Fleet would provide cover for Luzon north and General Kenney's land-based army planes would protect Mindoro and the Visayas south.

A slow and unwieldy group of navy and army tugs, barges, LCTs and an aviation tanker, known appropriately as the Slow Tow Convoy, was the first to leave Leyte Gulf, protected by three destroyers and two destroyer escorts at 0600 on December 12. This group was overtaken early on December by the main attack group, Admiral Struble's Mindoro Attack Force led by Nashville.

Early on the morning of December 13, 1944 Nashville cruised off the coast of Mindoro while twelve Navy fighters from escort carriers and thirty-five land-based Corsairs of Marine Air Group 12 provided cover overhead. At dawn that morning the ship's doctor told all hands to change to clean uniforms to cut down on risk of infection in case of wounds. At 0803 general quarters was sounded to repel an enemy air attack but no action occurred. However, the presence of the force was discovered sometime that morning, perhaps as early as 0900 by a Japanese reconnaissance plane. An undetermined time later, Japanese Val kamikaze bombers with fighter escorts took off from a Visayan airfield.

The Nashville sat almost directly in the center of the Task Group 78.3, well within the protective screen of destroyers but also within four short quick air miles from a tiny island off the southern end of Negros Island. The routine complement of 'Condition 2' (half crew on watch, half off) crew manned the guns and lookout stations while extra crew members were on deck to enjoy the weather. It was a travel poster Pacific day, electric blue skies with some low cloud cover and sporadic puffy, brilliantly white clouds floating about over an infinite horizon of deep blue sea and lush green islands, a strange dichotomy of beautiful Pacific scenery spotted with scores of harshly painted jagged warships. Crewman Fred Grider remembers Glenn Miller's "Tuxedo Junction" playing on the ship's intercom, no doubt bringing dreams of home, dances, girls, wives, moms and dads, and hopes to get back to that world the crew left, many as teenagers not out of high school.

Lieutenant John Powell Riley, Jr. left the bridge and proceeded down a ladder to the wardroom below the main deck in search of coffee, a drink he had quit many months ago. Billy Ray Liverly, experiencing the symptoms of the first and only cold he had ever had in his life, was persuaded by others to go below decks and seek something from the doc. Harry J. Grocki RM3c just finished his normal watch and went below decks to catch up on his sleep. Hugh D. Patrick went below decks for an unknown reason even to him at the time. Maury Jack Wood Ship Cook 1c was told at the last minute without explanation to switch shifts with another crewmember. Fate was playing an active hand that day.

At 1457, just as the Nashville was coming about the southern end of Negros Island, steaming towards the Sulu Sea, sharp-eyed lookouts spotted a Val single engine plane at 5,000 feet just over the island off the starboard side of the ship. The crew thought the ship astern was the target and indeed it appeared that way from the dive path of the plane. Crewmembers were thinking, "Oh God, they are going to get it if that plane gets through." But then in an instant the pilot banked so hard left that his wings were perpendicular to the water, and with that the fate of the Nashville and her crew was forever altered. Men watched in horror and disbelief as they could see bombs fastened on both wings as the plane bore down on them with every intention of killing as many of them as possible. Apparently aiming for the bridge, where nearly thirty officers and men were present, the tip of the right wing caught the end of a 40mm anti-aircraft gun port- side just aft and the plane slammed into the Nashville amidships at 400 miles an hour with an instant and powerful impact. The ship violently bolted and shuddered, the first evidence for the crew below decks that something had gone horribly wrong. The bomb on the right wing exploded ten feet above the port five-inch battery, sending a powerful shockwave and a deadly shrapnel spray across the deck, ripping through steel bulkheads, gun barrels, ammunition, decking, and human beings. The left wing broke loose and its bomb exploded ten feet above the starboard five-inch battery, shooting a violent concussion wave and hundreds of pieces of red-hot jagged shrapnel in all directions. Body parts, specks of flesh, fluids of both man and machine blew through doorways, along bulkheads, against men, and down hallways along much of the length of the ship.

Aviation gasoline spewed forth soaking men, ammunition, guns, and everything else before exploding in a millisecond, sending flames more than seventy feet forward and higher than the ship's smokestacks. Searing fires erupted from the foremast to the mainmast topside. The blast literally clogged the on deck blow intakes and momentarily knocked out the fires in the fireroom, but men like John. W. Bosier CMM ran topside, cleared the intakes, and relit the fires quickly.

Fires also erupted on the second deck, in the #2 fireroom, uptakes on the third deck, and in the superstructure as high as the signal bridge. The burning aviation fuel then ignited a five-inch ready ammunition box portside causing more deadly explosions. Still, the horror continued as the fifty-caliber machine gun ammunition from the Japanese plane exploded as did some of the ship's 20mm and 40mm ammunition, creating a deadly blast of bullets and shrapnel flying in all directions.

The scene on deck was nothing short of pure horror surpassing a man's worst nightmares. The Nashville was a vessel of death and destruction. Men were blown overboard. Men's bodies were penetrated by jagged searing hot metal fragments, limbs were torn from torsos, torsos from trunks, and some simply disintegrated in the concussion and fire. The ship itself fared no better than the crew. Large five-inch guns were twisted like putty, melted and put out of commission as were 40mm and 20mm guns amidships, the thirty-six-inch searchlights simply ceased to exist, the teak decks were shredded like toothpicks, bulkheads crushed and burnt, paint seared off, gun barrels twisted like straws.

A bomb or shell exploding on a ship kills and maims in multiple, horrible ways. The pressure of the blast itself attacks in a wave that crushes bodies, strips flesh and muscle from bone, and in some cases totally vaporizes human beings. It is not simply metal bomb fragments that also kill but the ship's own metal pieces blasted into tiny fragments, even liquefied that then pass through a man's body at hypersonic speed.

The memory of the attack remained seared into the minds of the survivors for the rest of their lives. James D. Baccus was stationed in Turret 1 for general quarters. "We had just come back from the Mess Hall and I was sitting on the deck inside the turret, playing Backgammon, when the ship shook and there was one hell of a noise. I then looked through the scuttle hole in the deck of the turret, where the shell cases are ejected to the ship's deck, and several sailors were crawling under the overhang for protection. They were bloody, some with legs and arms either gone or badly injured." Most of the men James saw would not survive.

"So many of my shipmates, some close friends dead and wounded. The wounds were so terrible, especially the burns," remembered William Smith, Chief Shipfitter.

Hugh D. Patrick and a buddy ran topside as soon as they realized what had happened and they immediately heard frantic pounding on a closed hatch. They opened the hatch and continued forward to see if they could help and then in essence rescued a doomed sailor. It was almost fifty years later that Frank Prentice tracked down Hugh to thank him for saving his life by opening that hatch.

GM3c Alfonso Garcia Vejar had just left his station as he was relieved and went below deck to eat. The man that took his place was killed instantly. Alfonso was alive by sheer chance and fate.

James Clark received a Purple Heart as a result of the attack, "I was stationed in a 40mm gun director with a guy named Johnson when the kamikaze attack occurred, the plane hit directly below us. Our gun crew, which was one level below and closer to the plane, was hit hard.

Later, after all the fires were out I was back at my station and witnessed a Marine near the top of the ladder who was so badly wounded his body was just a heap and his clothing was smoldering. I didn't know how this man could be alive. When a Marine officer approached him he held out his hand and said, 'help me sir.' I know that Marine officer has had many nightmares about that incident and I can still see it."

The blast blew men into bulkheads, across the deck and through doorways. Ed Roiek MM1 was blown clear through two doorways yet managed to survive.

"I was told to switch the shift with one of my shipmates," said Maury Jack Wood, Ship Cook 1c. "The kamikaze hit the ship where a shipmate took my shift. He was killed and it should have been me. I will never forget this as long as I live. I have shared this information with my family."

Those that were below decks were lucky and they knew it. John J. Cotton SK2c said, "I am here because I was in a repair party below decks."

Young Edward "Bulldog" Remler rushed into the overcrowded Sick Bay to help the doctors and medics any way he could. Wounded, dead, and dieing were piling up in the corridor as if they were coming off an assembly line. Horribly mangled men all about, screams of agony, groans, vomiting, blood mixed with body fluids of all sorts pooling up to his ankles, the sound of anti-aircraft guns firing and exploding ammunition decks above him formed a Kaleidoscope memory in his mind, never to fully leave him. Incredibly, there was another memory to return even more forcefully in his future. Bulldog had to hold men down while limbs were amputated, sometimes without full anesthesia. After the first amputation the doctor told him to take the severed leg of a sailor. Bulldog burst out, "What do you want me to do with it?" and was promptly told to toss it into a corner where others were beginning to form a sizeable pile. Nearly fifty years later, at one of the ship's reunions, he spotted a one-legged man in a wheelchair, someone he had not seen at any prior reunion. It was of course that first sailor he held. They became fast friends and at times traveled together on vacations and to reunions.

For everyone involved, it was the worst day of their navy lives, their entire lives in some ways, and certainly the worst navy duty they ever had. Writing letters to the families of Marines killed in the attack was the worst duty for Rufus B. Thompson, Lt. Colonel USMC. "My assistant, 2nd Lt. Paul Finn Pederson, and 1st Sergeant Alton B. Chambers and I were the only ones in the detachment not wounded or killed. Pederson was stationed forward and I was stationed aft and Chambers was in charge of the 40mm batteries on the fantail."

Richard Metcalf was among the seriously wounded, "I lay on the deck of the ship with the other wounded and dying with blood pouring from my severely wounded arm, amid the terrible screams and cries for help of the injured and dying sailors (some still on fire and others burned to a crisp), with the air we were breathing filled with the stench of burning flesh mixed with burning fuel and ammunition and further mixed with vomit of ill shipmates from the horror facing them. I was only nineteen years of age at the time. When the medics were going to operate on my arm they said expect to find my arm had been amputated but they would try to save it. They had run out of morphine and shoved a spoon in my mouth and told me to bite on it so I could endure the pain."

Fred Grider never forgot the nightmare, "My buddy and I had just been relieved of duty in CIC (Combat Information Center) and we were proceeding aft on the starboard side as the Captain finished telling everyone about the upcoming operation. Glenn Miller's record of "Tuxedo Junction" was playing on the PA system. I told my friend, Harry Shevers RM2c to hurry with me to the hanger deck where we were bunked and just as we were about halfway down the ladder the kamikaze hit. About fifteen minutes later we went topside and carried the wounded to Aid Areas. A few hours later I was transferred to the destroyer Sashiled with the rest of our SAC Group except the two that had relieved my friend Harry and me. One of our buddies, Eddy English RM2c was killed instantly and his lifelong friend Dor Cosgrove RM2c died a few days later."

Alex Zdurne had enlisted with his older brother, straight from the farm. When the four Sullivan brothers, serving aboard the same ship, were killed earlier in the war, the Navy instituted a policy to prevent such a tragedy from occurring again, and asked Alex and his brother to split up. A coin was tossed and his brother was transferred off the ship. His gun duty station was one of the ones hit by the kamikaze. He surely would have died in the attack, literally having his life saved by a coin toss. Alex was assigned to a damage control party. His area sustained heavy damage due to shrapnel and fire and had live ammunition covered with smoke and fire. Alex assisted the executive officer in bringing fire fighting equipment to the area, bravely ignoring the red hot ammunition and fire. He then was ordered to the captain's cabin to evacuate staff but on his way ammunition exploded wounding him, but he carried on his duty and removed wounded personnel. He received a Bronze Star and Purple Heart for his actions as did others this fateful, horrific day. Alex actually refused receiving the Purple Heart because such a medal involves notification of parents and he did not want to worry or shock his parents who were not in good health. A most thoughtful consideration.

Billie Ray Liverly noted "I had just been relieved from my battle station and was going to the Communications Deck to sleep and rest (at times men could sleep on deck in the hot tropical heat). However, I had somewhat of a cold at the time and I debated whether to go below deck to rest or lay on the Communications Deck. I did decide the wind would be too much and did go below deck. It was at this time that the Japanese suicide plane hit the Nashville amidships. I immediately came up on deck to go to my battle station when I saw sailors and shipmates hanging over the anti-aircraft batteries, dead, many wounded. All the sailors on the Communications Deck were killed by shrapnel. I was told to help where I could so I went to help the wounded get to the large Chief Petty Officer's Quarters for treatment of burns, etc. At this point I was asked to, and had prayers with numerous shipmates, and they would hold my hand, squeeze and look up at me and smile. They would say 'thanks Billy Ray'."

"We were steaming with a convoy to support a landing on Mindoro Island. We were in Condition 2, half the crew on watch and half off. I was off watch, in my rack trying to get some rest. I remember the sound as "kerrump." I grabbed my clothes and headed for my battle station in No. 2 Fireroom. We continued on with the convoy but were ordered to transfer the attacking group commander and his staff to another ship and to return to Leyte Gulf. After securing from watch I went topside to see what the damage was. Quite a bit of midships. The deck around Number 4 and 5 Turrets was covered with bodies. Our chief engineer was among them. The wounded were transferred to hospitals and the bodies were sent ashore," noted Charles L. Norman WT1c.

Paul Taloff PWM1c, like many others, did the critical but gruesome task of taking care of their shipmates, "I was on the bridge when he hit us. I dropped down from the range finder and began to tend to the wounded."

Joseph A. Graves SM2c exhibited the bravery of his shipmates that day, "I was a very lucky person. For once I paid attention to the announcement over the PA system to stay below decks, wear caps and long sleeve shirts. Fred Walters and I had just got through with chow after being relieved from watch at noontime. We were reading up in the Marine quarters when we heard the explosion. We rushed for our battle stations up through the captain's passageway when I opened the hatch to the main deck. There it was right in front of me, fire, exploding ammunition, people burned to a crisp. Fred and I helped to get the injured inside and down to Sick Bay. After that we grabbed the water hose and helped put out the fire. We did not get to our battle station until after dark that night."

John W. Bosler was below decks in the oppressive heat of a fireroom, "I was in No. 3 Fireroom as Fireroom Repairman and had to have everybody leave the fireroom until I checked forced draft fan blowers."

"The worst thing was the explosion and the shaking of the ship," said Bill Banks BM1c. "Also the smell of death, the smoke, dust, and whatever the air blower blew into the No. 1 Fireroom. Also, trying to keep the steam pressure at 440# pressure. Above all was being asked to identify the dead bodies on the top deck. You never get rid of that smell of blood and death. But every man was faithful to his post." That distinctive smell stayed with Bill Banks, George Bustin, and everyone else that experienced it for the rest of their lives.

Bob Shafer was awakened from an afternoon nap. "My buddy Jim Von and I were taking a nap up in sky control. It was a beautiful day. When the crash came we didn't know what it was at first. My buddy leaned over the shield to look, with both hands on the shield, and the shrapnel from the 25mm guns that were on fire down below, that shrapnel cut his fingers off at the base where he had them over that shield. It happened so fast, he pulled his hands back and they were all bloody and I said what in the world happened to you? He said I got my hands all shot up. Then I looked over the shield and all I could see was fire and shrapnel and blood.

You heard the expression a river of blood? I don't know why but that was the first thing that came into my mind, it was terrible."

Even former Nashvillers like Clarence D. Bivins, FC3c, experienced the kamikaze hit.

"I was aboard the Nashville from Nov 39 to June 42. In 1944 I was on the USS Maryland and was on the fire control tower when a couple of friends and I observed the kamikaze attack. At that time I had no idea how bad it was!"

It was one horrible imprinted memory after another for the crew. Harry J. Grocki RM3c remembers, "The USMC was wiped out on their gun deck and I saw one Marine just standing there with his guts hanging out."

Many men received medals for heroic action, including J. R. Clifton who was awarded a Bronze Star for his actions after the kamikaze attack.

Incredibly, the crew responded instantly and without any thought of personal safety as men of all ranks and divisions raced to help the wounded and dieing and fight the fires ravaging the ship. In roughly ninety seconds the "fog fighting" equipment was manned on the scene. Fifteen hoses were on the scene topside in less than five minutes. Fires on all decks were contained in less than ten minutes and were completely extinguished in less than twenty minutes, a remarkable achievement amid massive death, burning flesh, body parts, and exploding ammunition. Without a doubt, according to the official US Navy reports, the ship itself was saved by the heroics of her crew. Sadly, many of the crew could not be saved.

Robert L. Shafer BM2c ran into the carnage as part of a firefighting crew putting water on the red hot ammunition boxes, and received a commendation for rescuing one of the young sailors hiding from the exploding ammunition and fires in one of those ammunition boxes. Shafer was wounded when a flash explosion temporarily blinded him in both eyes. "You did your job not thinking. You helped put out fires not thinking you could get killed. Your buddies needed your help so that is what you did."

The explosion sent several men straight into the sea. "The next thing I remember is hitting the water," said Arvel F. Gearing, Sr., GM. "There were five sailors in the water, three sailors from our five-inch gun,

gun #6. I did not have a life jacket of my own and when I found three life jackets in the water I gave them all away to other sailors. I found another life jacket. At about the same time, I saw an arm come up out of the water. By this time, my own hands were stiff due to my own serious wounds and burns, so I took the life jacket in my teeth and swam over to that sailor. I told him to clamp the lifejacket under his arm and I would pull him over to the rest of the crew. I thought it was best for all of us to stay together in case a rescue ship came along. Eventually a minesweeper picked us up." Arvel's extraordinary bravery and unselfish actions were common.

Robert G. Barton CCS repeatedly entered the fire area amidst exploding ammunition and carried wounded men on his back to safety. Once he was seen carrying two men on his back at one time. Barton himself had thirty wounds on his body including a severed toe, but he did not seek medical attention until he had saved as many men as could be done. One wonders where such men come from, how do human beings do such things?

Despite having the fingertips on his right hand blown off, James M. Vaughn, on his own initiative, organized an emergency gun crew to man a flak gun against further incoming enemy planes.

Navigator Commander Robert H. Taylor was in the plot room at the moment of impact, sitting on a stool while he routinely plotted a course change. With the sudden impact and explosions came hundreds of pieces of thin shrapnel flying across the deck, and three officers were dead just outside of the chart room. Taylor raced to the bridge to report to Captain Coney and noticed intense flames near the ready racks inside the shield of the portside 40mm near the bridge. It was none other than the trainer of all of Nashville's fire fighting crews, Lieutenant Commander Leonard E. Meyer that responded to Taylor's summons with a crew that he led personally to extinguish the flames and end the threat.

Murlin Spencer was an Associated Press War Correspondent and filed a report that included the following, but it did not appear in stateside papers until the following June as was frequently the practice during the war.

"Sailors race by to grab hoses piled neatly on deck and haul them back towards the bridge. In an incredibly short time they thread their way up ladders to points of vantage from which to fight the fire."

"As they pour water on the flames, there comes a series of smaller explosions and you know the fire has touched off the ammunition stacked by the anti-aircraft guns. Tracer shells scream crazily in every direction but the firemen stand their ground. As do the gunners and the guns still in firing condition bark revengeful at a twin-engine bomber seeking to bore in from the north. They drive it off and you feel better because there is still a lot of fight left in the ship and the men who sail her."

"As the flames subside and the black smoke turns to gray, more wounded come forward. One is a doctor and he has more courage than any man I ever saw. They carry him back in a wire litter and he is conscious and rational. His big bulk fills the upper half of the litter but the deck shows through the wire mesh where his legs are supposed to be. Another doctor hurries to him and the wounded officer talks as though he had much to say in a short time. 'They will be dependent,' you catch that part of it. The big man raises himself up and takes one look down. There is no expression on his face. He stops a passing sailor and asks, 'Are we fighting them off?'"

"Little streams of blood trickle along the cracks in the deck. There are many more wounded now and the wardroom below is filling as fast as the uninjured can lower them down the steep ladders. You remember the words of a gunner who told you the day before, 'We have six purple hearts on this ship.' He said it to show his ship had been in action. There will be many times that number now. Who are these men? I took no names because they are all heroes—those that died by their guns, those who lived to fight the fire and the Japanese, those wounded who did their job as long as they could. That is what it is like when a great ship is hit. As dusk falls the Nashville moves on. She is still a fighting ship and she holds her place in line and the war goes on.'"

The firefighting and damage control crews along with the rest of the crew saved the ship with their unselfish sacrifice. Lieutenant Commander Leonard E. Meyer had trained all of the firefighting crew and even personally led a detail of men to fight a fire at an ammunition box that could easily have exploded and instantly killed them all. Everyone at every rank and duty station did all they could to save their ship and their buddies without regard to their own mortality.

Albert L. Pender MM1c was asleep at the time but that does not mean he was completely spared the horror of the attack. He was soon picking up the dead and wounded and pieces thereof, as were many others like him.

At 1458, amid the height of the fires, explosions, and death, general quarters was sounded to repel air attacks with the few anti-aircraft guns functioning and the surviving crew manned their battle stations as training and duty dictated. At 1507, just eleven minutes after the attack and amid the heroic firefighting of the crew, surviving anti-aircraft crews commenced firing at Japanese aircraft flying low beyond the destroyer screen. Firing ceased at 1508. Nashville was seriously wounded but continued to fight. She maneuvered violently until such time as destroyer Stanly, assigned the duty of helping crippled ships, closed enough to render assistance. Minesweeper YMS-315 worked to pick up men blown overboard.

The kamikaze attack killed 133 men, including four initially missing, and wounded another 190, almost a third of the entire crew of the ship. Heroism was common. Nearly sixty citations were issued (and be sure more could have been) for heroism. Some men refused them, not out of disrespect, but rather in respect of those brave men that died and others seriously injured, many while coming to the aid of their crewmates.

Even after the fires were extinguished, the wounded attended to and the dead removed in body bags to the fantail, the horror continued for some of the crew. Joseph A. Graves SM2c was among those assigned to clean up the ship as best could done under the circumstances, as he so understates "scraping and washing the overhead and bulkheads, cleaning the fragments of bone, hair, and blood and guts of your shipmates was no easy task."

Emil Machrone was in Turret 1 during the impact and thought the ship had been struck by a torpedo. But soon officers were sending out the call for each turret to send two men to help move the dead and wounded from the deck, Machrone's turret sent two sixteen- year-old sailors for the duty but soon they were back in the turret, shaking and crying at the carnage they had encountered. They were quickly sent below and twenty-eight-year- old Machrone and another "older" sailor were volunteered for the duty. They were given rubber gloves that covered them to the elbow and sent on their way. The first casualty he came to had his stomach and other organs completely outside of his body. The Lieutenant said, "Get a hold of yourself, you have to clean these guys up, just put his stomach back into his body and place him in the bag." Machrone did it, of course. Eventually, all the bodies or recognizable parts thereof were placed near the stern and in the hanger. Machrone saluted them and went back to his duty in Turret #1.

Joe Mills was another sailor with an unimaginable duty to perform, "Jerry (Chaplain Gerald Smith) and I went over to the starboard side and I hate to say this but we found guys over there that were blown in half and bodies all over the place and we were always told to get the ship in shape for battle, so Jerry and I would find the dogtags and Jerry would say prayers over them and then we would push them over the side and bury them at sea. Well, we found out they wanted them back on the fantail, so after two fellas we stopped that thing. But I'll never forget that day, Jerry's praying and I'm finding the dogtags. We tried to get things cleaned up. It was a mess."

But a full week after the kamikaze hit there remained the smell of "death" throughout the ventilation systems of the ship, as was to be expected. Even so, there was an absolutely overpowering stench in the mess hall itself. As it turned out, one sailor previously thought missing or his body obliterated in the blast was neither. He had been blown down the airshaft and right through the protective screening. What was left of him simply began to rot in the tropic heat. Once his remains were found and removed, the mystery stench dissipated in time, but for many the mess hall was never the same.

Chief Shipfitter William Smith was at his battle station between Turret 3 and the Ward Room on the second deck. In times as these the Ward Room was designated as the Main Battle Dressing Station. "The wounded were passed down to us and we carried them into the Ward Room. I helped carry Commander Beach into the Ward Room. Both legs were blown off at his thighs. I was at his head on the stretcher and he kept saying, 'Well, they got me,' and I kept trying to reassure him, but of course he died. His last thoughts were of his wife and children. He started saying, 'please take care of my wife and children,' and I kept trying to tell him he was going to be taking care of them, but he knew better".

Nashville was still full of fight and had her anti-aircraft guns in action ten minutes after the kamikaze attack, fending off yet another enemy air attack on the convoy. She continued steaming with the rest of the convoy for several more hours as command was transferred and her Army-Navy invasion staff was taken off ship. But due to the "unusually extensive" damage, including the total destruction of her CIC (Combat Information Center) and Communication Office she was ordered to return to Leyte Gulf. On her way to Leyte the Japanese sent a destroyer specifically to hunt and sink Nashville while she was so deeply wounded, but an American destroyer caught the Japanese ship and the hunter became the hunted and was promptly sunk.

With the destroyer escorting them Nashville steamed on to Leyte and actually received a mail delivery that Joe Mills definitely found interesting. "When we got hit with the kamikaze that day, we came back that night, we had a destroyer with us. We got back into Leyte Gulf and we picked up our mail. I was a junior officer of the watch on the bridge. The Quartermaster came up to me and says, 'I've got some orders here for you,' and the mail we hadn't picked up were my orders back to the States."

At Tacloban, the seriously wounded of the 190 men were taken ashore for hospitalization and the 133 dead officers and men were removed and buried in a military cemetery. Some temporary repairs were able to be made at Seeadler Harbor but Nashville was so extensively and seriously damaged as to need major repairs. Christmas Day 1944 was unlike any other the ship or crew had experienced, Nashville began her mournful 12,000 mile journey to Puget Sound Navy Yard, Washington via Pearl Harbor. Nashville left Pearl Harbor on January 6, 1945 in the company of battleship USS Alabama. With deckplates and bulkheads still buckled and blackened, and smokestacks, bulkheads, and guns riddled with bomb fragments, and her undefeated and scorched ensign flying proudly, she made her way into the Puget Sound Navy Yard in Bremerton, Washington on January 12.

General MacArthur going ashore, Philippines

General MacArthur ashore, Philippines

USS Nashville offshore, Philippines

General MacArthur aboard Nashville

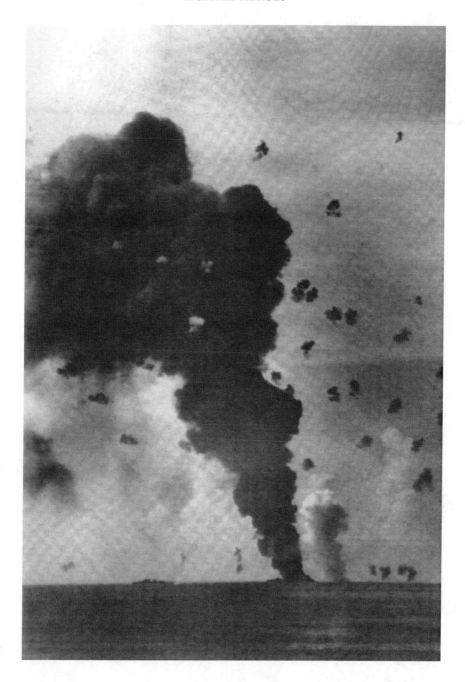

Nashville is hit

Kamikaze damage amidship

Kamikaze damage to 5" portside gun

Kamikaze wounded being transferred for treatment

Some of the Kamikaze dead port side, stern

More Kamikaze dead starboard side, stern

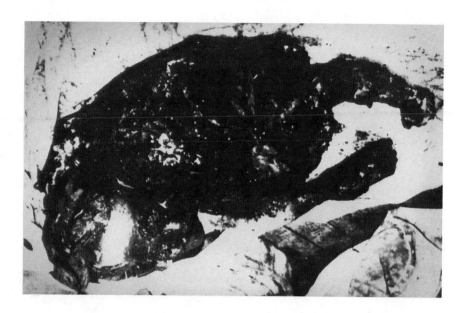

Remains of dead Kamikaze pilot

CHAPTER 9
Repair: Return and Fight

***

"It was hard to look at her all torn up like that. I had tears in my eyes. She had been my home for over three and a half years."
-George L. Bustin

***

Nashville had no sooner docked than twenty-four hour efforts were underway to patch her wounds and make her fully battle ready again. The war continued and she was needed. Nashville took her place in a specially constructed "cradle" for capital ships. Around the clock, seven days a week, repairs and modernization by civilian and Navy personnel alike continued for two months as some of the crew were transferred to other duties with the remaining crew and green replacements received training in all the facets of crewing a fighting ship being prepared to return to battle, including the anticipated invasion of the Japanese home islands.

As was the usual practice when a ship takes a devastating hit like Nashville did and is docked for an extended period to perform extensive repairs, a good deal of the crew is rotated on and off the ship, especially many old salt veterans that had served for years. Richard Smith was one of the new guys coming aboard the war scarred ship. "Six of my classmates and I were recent graduates of Fire Control and Gunnery schools and had been assigned to the USS Nashville. Scuttlebutt was that casualties among Fire Controlmen and Gunners Mates was extremely heavy," and so it was. A ship is more than a duty assignment, more than a place to work and sleep; it is a home full of memories as rich as any building on land, and it was not easy for many men to leave Nashville. George Bustin, GM2c was among them, "I went down to the dock to see the ship one last time. It was hard to look at her all torn up like that. I had tears in my eyes. She had been my home for over three and a half years."

Repairs were harrowing and difficult work. There was a shortage of "riggers," creating a bottleneck in the shipyard, with only three available for removing the twisted metal debris as it was cut away from the ship. Undaunted, shipfitters manhandled chunks or twisted superstructure metal down the gangways with brute strength. Further expediting repairs was the foresight and planning of Lieutenant Commander Leonard Meyer, the man that had trained the Nashville firefighting crews and had led a crew himself in fighting the kamikaze inferno. Meyer had previously flown to the navy yard with photographs and descriptions of the damage, thus saving critical time in getting the ship repaired and back into the war effort.

By March 4, 1945, four days before the end of the war in Europe, Nashville, now under the command of Captain Atherton Macondray, Jr., was conducting sea trials and training off the Washington coast. Richard Smith said, "We made several trips out to Puget Sound and the ship would vibrate noticeably when at full throttle. At the end of our final run we reached the required top knot speed in both directions. I was sitting in a straight chair, leaning against the bulkhead in Control II several decks up and writing a letter. I suddenly realized the ship was making a very sharp turn and heeling considerably. As a 'boot' sailor I wondered if we were going to tip over. We had run over a stray log from a nearby logging operation and it had wedged between the port screws, stopping them instantly and sending the ship into an uncontrolled turn." More repairs were in order after that unfortunate episode and then she left the northwest and arrived in sunny San Diego just in time to see Howard Hughes "Spruce Goose" taxing in the harbor with all eight engines going and then of course, more sea trials and drills. San Diego was another good liberty town for many of the men. James D. "Buddy" Backus and friends enjoyed it immensely. "Our crazy gang went over for liberty and as usual got drunk. John Morrissey would walk up to some good looking girl and ask her if she knew what happened to Robin Hood while walking through Sherwood Forest, and she would say 'no,' then he would say, 'a great big bear bit her in the ass just like this,' and he would bite her in the ass, just another crazy antic."

Richard A. Smith went for the usual liberty without incident but it was interesting coming back to the Nashville anchored in the harbor with many other ships, rather than tied up at a dock. "The fog was so thick you could not see the ship until you were within a few feet of it. We put out from shore in tenders. Each ship rang the ship's bell to sound out the ship's number—Nashville sounded four bells then three bells for CL-43, meanwhile sounding the ship's foghorn. We then proceeded in the direction of the familiar number of bell sounds until close enough for more positive identification. That was certainly the densest, thickest fog I had ever seen." Nashville continued training off San Diego, repair patches still visible under the paint, during April 4-13, 1945.

By April 15 she was ready to go and set sail for more action in the Western Pacific. Continuing training as she headed back to war, Nashville stopped in Pearl Harbor April 21-30. While in Hawaii the ship welcomed many new crew members and conducted training exercises for ship and crew. Some of the new crew were green officers as Richard Smith particularly noticed during one exercise: "One of the most important shipboard rules is that above the main deck you go up the ladders on the portside and down the ladders on the starboard side of the ship. I had to go from the aft AA Director to the forward Main Battery Director when general quarters sounded. One did not walk down the down ladders, leaning forward and grasping the siderails halfway down, then swinging your legs through and landing at the bottom of the ladder, all in one motion. I was halfway down a ladder to the second deck one day, ready to swing my legs through when I realized that an officer was starting up the ladder. Too late to stop, I swung through, my knees struck him full in the chest and he toppled backwards to the deck below. I recall seeing his white officer's cap rolling across the deck, but I kept going to the next ladder. He probably never knew who or what hit him, but I'm sure he learned never to go up a 'down' ladder again." Leaving Hawaii, Nashville steamed on to familiar Seeadler Harbor and Leyte Gulf on her way to her order destination of Subic Bay, Luzon, Philippines on May 16. She entered Subic Bay at night, carefully, slowly sailing past the numerous sunken and partially sunken ships in the harbor, all marked by a white light for range-finding navigation purposes. By May 21 she was once again a flagship under Rear Admiral Berkey for Task Force 74 and steamed into Brunei Bay on Borneo's northwest coast on June 7.

***

Tarakan, Borneo
(April-July 45)

By April 1945, with the defeat of Nazi Germany, Churchill and the British were somewhat eager to get in on the war in the Pacific where they had been necessarily a minor force since battleship HMS Prince of Wales and battlecruiser HMS Repulse were sunk off Singapore on December 8, 1945. Borneo and surrounding islands seemed a suitable place to start. While most of Borneo had been a Dutch protectorate, the northern coast and offshore islands such as Tarakan and Brunei had been a British protectorate. Borneo had oil fields that had been feeding the Japanese war effort since they invaded the territory in January 1942. The American Joint Chiefs of Staff wanted the British Navy to handle the invasion of Borneo with Australian troops. It all made so much good sense. But the British, once they were advised of American plans for Olympic and Coronet to invade Japan by the end of 1945, wanted to apply their presence to the big show against the enemy home islands. And since the naval forces of the Netherlands had all but ceased to exist, it of course fell upon the United States and specifically Nashville and the Seventh Fleet to handle the job. The British wanted to save their naval resources for the anticipated invasion of Japan so Nashville got the Borneo job as a result of international politics.

There were valuable oilfields on heart-shaped Tarakan and an airfield. It was a small island at fifteen miles long by eleven miles at its widest point. It was heavily mined in the waters, had a small beach 200 yards long, and was about to join a long list of Japanese held islands that would be introduced to the United States Navy by a heavy bombardment of Nashville's and other's six-inch shells. Nashville and crew, at least the veterans on board, took the operation in stride and performed without incidence or exception.

***

Brunei Bay, Borneo
(June 45)

After Tarakan the next Borneo target on the list of General MacArthur's plan was Brunei Bay, a large natural harbor on the north coast of the island. Once again, Nashville and the other cruisers of Admiral Berkey's group, Phoenix, Boise, and HMAS Hobart and seven destroyers were chosen to soften the Japanese defenses prior to Allied troops (in this case Australian) storming the beaches. Z-Day, as designated by MacArthur, was June 10, so Nashville and the other ships of Berkey's group arrived offshore on June 8 to cover minesweeping operations conducted on the eighth and ninth prior to the invasion. Nashville covered the minesweepers as they snuck in under the guns of the Japanese and destroyed minefields, and then Nashville opened up during the next two days, bombarding Japanese positions in a manner that McArthur described as "one of mathematical precision." The bombardment was so effective that the Japanese rapidly retreated into the interior, allowing Aussie troops to land without resistance.

On June 10 Nashville, Phoenix, Boise, and Hobart commenced bombardment at 0805 and 0815 on the two landing beaches. The landings were unopposed. The Navy had done its job well once again. Captain H.B. Hudson, in charge of local troop operations, sent the following message to Admiral Royal who was in charge of all naval operations for the Borneo campaign: "On the eve of your departure, I wish to express admiration and appreciation of the thorough, efficient, and gallant and successful manner in which the naval forces under your command carried out its vital role in both the Borneo operations."

On June 17, as resistance on Brunei had been minimized, Nashville set sail for Tawi Tawi Island in the Sulu Archipelago where she stayed for five days and then made a short voyage for an even shorter stay at Puerto Princesa on Palawan Island. Alex Zdurne sent home the letter the Navy gave out after a campaign, all nicely typed with a blank space for the sailor or Marine to write in the recipient name(s) and one for the serviceman's sign off and signature. For the Brunei Bay action the letter was not all that different from others before and later.

"Aboard the USS Nashville somewhere in the Philippines."
"Dear _____
I am now permitted to tell you that our ship was a part of the task force which covered the amphibious landings in Brunei Bay on the northwest coast of Borneo early last month. We steamed into Brunei Bay three days before D-Day to cover the fleet of U.S. minesweepers which were delousing the bay of Jap mines and you would really go

for these gallant little craft who slipped into the shores and inlets under the very noses of the Japs, destroying minefields, exploding floating mines and charting the channels. The next day we opened a bombardment of enemy positions and gun installations and the Nashville proved she had lost none of the fine gunnery skill for which she is noted. From our position off shore we could observe the points under fire and a Jap ammunition dump was seen to explode and points that were once Japanese positions were leveled. So thorough and methodical was our bombardment that when the "Aussie" troops, the famed "Desert Rats" of North Africa, landed on D-Day they were almost unmolested, the Jap forces having fled to the hills of the interior. General Douglas MacArthur, Commander-in-Chief, U.S. Army forces in the Pacific, witnessed the landings and commended the force and its personnel with a "Well done." The rich Borneo oilfields near Brunei Bay produce a very fine grade of oil and are considered one of the finest prizes of the Pacific War. Apparently the Japanese set fire to these in their flight as we could see the fires from the oilfields at night. An observation party of officers and enlisted men found Labuan Island very interesting when they went ashore a few days later. There were many coconuts and tropical fruits including bananas, mangos, etc., and apparently at one time a development or project had been started there. The main roads, although very narrow, were paved and had deep concrete gutters on each side. They also had electric street lamps, although there were very few houses along the roads. Our mail was flown to Brunei arriving on D-Day plus one and by the end of the week recreation parties were going ashore on a small island that was located in the entrance of the bay. The "Aussies" had found three or four Japs there and apparently the place had been used as an observation post and a weather station by the Japs. The island was small, but interesting with its tropical trees which provided a shady spot, as well as a nice place for a swim."

"Restricted to family and friends only-not for publication."

And the war continued on.

***

Balikpapan

Although it was not known at the time since planning for operations Coronet and Olympic, the invasion of Japan was in full process, the amphibious invasion of Balikpapan was to be the last such major invasion during the war. The Japanese had occupied Balikpapan on January 23, 1942 for the same reason they occupied other Borneo locations, oil. Once again Nashville, carrying the flag of Admiral Berkey arrived off the coast with three escort carriers, five other American cruisers, two Australian and one Dutch cruiser, and an assortment of destroyers. At just before sunrise at 0700 hours July 1, under a low broken overcast, Nashville and the rest of the task force commenced a two hour bombardment against the island. The bombardment in conjunction with aerial bombing from the planes off the escort carriers delivered 38,052 shells, 3,000 tons of bombs, 7,361 rockets, and 114,000 rounds of automatic weapons fire. It was no accident that the Australian troops going ashore did so without a single casualty, over 460 Japanese dead were found on and near the landing beaches.

Besides shelling the beach and surrounding areas, Nashville also had a hand in providing spotting services with her aircraft. Gerald T. Jones, AMM3c was part of the crew that was responsible for the upkeep and operations of the planes. "We lowered a plane over the side with our second flight officer aboard. He flew around the point, rendezvoused with the ships, and spotted for them. After shelling was complete, he mistakenly decided to fly overland instead of flying around the point. During the flight he took a 40mm AK-AK through the left wing. It didn't disable the plane but he did get some shrapnel in the cockpit. Since the ship was not moving, and being slightly wounded, he landed too hot and banged into the back of the ship. We got him and the plane back on board but I had a heck of a time getting my airplane repaired and back in the air."

As the Australians moved inland Nashville and the other cruisers and destroyers hit strongpoint targets on request, much to the satisfaction of the Australians. This call-fire support continued for several days. On July 4, in honor of Independence Day, Nashville, Phoenix, and five destroyers fired a twenty-one-gun salute to America. It so happened that the salute was aimed at a Japanese position on the island and the result was a magazine explosion and the cheering of the Aussies who loved to frequently call for cruiser and destroyer fire support day and night. There requests were always cheerfully granted by the US Navy.

On July 6 at 1911 hours Nashville again responded to an Aussie request for pinpoint shelling of a nest of Japanese machine guns. At ranges of 11,000-12,000 yards, Nashville rained three salvos of ninety-eight six-inch shells on the Japanese gunners on two targets, eliminating the Japanese and their guns. Request for support fire and rapid and effective response occurred regularly and methodically. But Nashville used more than her guns to help the Aussies and keep the Japanese on the run. Her aircraft dropped six Mark thirty, 100-pound bombs on enemy artillery and machine gun positions. During the course of this action one plane received damage from enemy AA fire but both plane and pilot returned safely to the ship.

By July 7 the Aussies had the situation well in hand ashore and Nashville set course and departed at 1022 steaming at twenty knots and returned to Tawi Tawi for inspection to determine the source of a vibration in her stern section. While waiting in Brunei Bay the Nashville was visited each morning and evening by a lone Japanese plane circling in the distance, just enough to send ship and crew to general quarters. This got old after a few days and the Nashville decided to take action, albeit not exactly textbook action. Richard A. Smith said, "Our flight crews rigged a couple of bombs to one of our planes and the pilot catapulted off to find the Japanese runway and put bomb craters in it to prevent any more take-offs by our tormentor. Our pilot flew very low so as not to miss the target and was riddled by small arms fire. He returned safely to the ship and reached the landing mat before the plane settled in the water, full of bullet holes. As the crane raised the plane to the main deck level we could see that the cockpit canopy had been shattered and the pilot suffered superficial face lacerations. Water spouted from the bullet holes in the pontoon and wings, etc. like a tin can. Fortunately the pilot was not seriously injured, but the plane made a mess of the hanger space and must have been a total loss. I don't know if the pilot had been successful in grounding our Japanese tormentor, but I don't recall any more dawn and dusk flights." Meanwhile, after a thorough inspection, the source of the vibration was never found and in fact the ship was declared in good condition, so after Rear Admiral Berkey departed Nashville July 16 at Subic Bay the ship and crew spent the next two weeks practicing gunnery and tactics in an attempt to stay sharp for coming battles.

The only ship damage during the operation was to the brave little minesweepers clearing the landing site of hundreds of mines. Even minesweepers can set off a mine and in some cases they did in this operation and were sunk or damaged. One such minesweeper carried mail that was destined, or at least addressed for Nashville. Richard Smith remembers, "We got word the mail boat was coming. We were at general quarters and I rushed to direct my range finder scopes to the mouth of the bay to get a closer look. The 'mail boat' was a minesweeper and before we were able to get a clear focus it struck a floating mine and exploded in flames. Apparently all aboard were killed and most of the mail was lost. I received parts of four or five letters that were badly water stained and mostly unreadable."

CHAPTER 10
The End of the War: New Duty

***

"Citizens were shooting off fireworks in joyous celebration. Then, and only then, did I think about going home, and it was a great feeling."
-Richard A. Smith

***

Plans for ending the war had been in play for many months. More and more ships were hovering around Subic Bay and other locations as the buildup continued. What was evident to most sailors and Marines was that something big was going on, something very big, big enough to push for an end to the war. Naturally, everyone thought that would be a massive invasion of the Japanese home islands by all branches of the American military as well as Australian and British and a long list of other Allies wanting to get in on the action of what was essentially an American operation. Richard A. Smith remembers the rumors and spending a few days at sea on practicing maneuvers for what everyone thought would be the great invasion. But then Nashville and the rest of the task force were ordered back to Subic Bay. Then on July 29, Nashville and the rest of Task Force 74 anchored in Subic Bay received emergency orders at 0000 hours to get underway at 0300 to intercept and engage a reported Japanese convoy steaming off the coast of Indochina. Nashville, along with USS San Francisco, Phoenix, Wiley, Haraden, Hart, Stevens, and HMAS Shropshire, Hobart, Bataan, and Warramunga set course at 240 degrees and steamed into the darkness at 21 knots. Later, changing course slightly, Task Force 74 was joined by USS New Orleans, Burns, and Bell at 0940. Shortly thereafter on the same day Nashville received a report for Task Force 74 to return to Subic Bay and they did, thus anti-climatically and unknowingly ending Nashville's last official sortie of the war. While she conducted training during the next few weeks there was to be no more steaming to bombard Japanese held islands or to engage or discourage the Imperial Japanese Navy and protect Allied ships, men, and material. History was soon to intervene in Nashville's wartime tenure.

The August 11, 1945 Nashville War Diary noted in part: "Received radio press reports of a Japanese offer to surrender. All hands to report in stride and continue to be on the alert for surprise attack." After years of war action Nashville and crew were not about to let down their guard for unconfirmed rumors. Then it came. On August 15, 1945 Nashville and crew heard the news they had been fighting for since Pearl Harbor, "Received official word of surrender of Japan and an order to cease offensive action." After many thousands of miles, hundreds of thousands of rounds of shells fired, in tropical heat and artic cold, after almost a 40% casualty rate, and after many fresh and eager boys dressed in sailor and Marine uniforms became men before their time, the war was finally and unconditionally over. Even so, at least 500 Japanese officers committed suicide rather than surrender. The head of the Japanese "Special Attack" forces, Ugaki, former Chief of Staff for Admiral Yamamoto, led eleven planes on one last wasteful kamikaze mission against the American Fleet off Okinawa. Three planes returned with engine trouble, saving the lives of the crews since all remaining planes were unceremoniously shot down without loss of America life.

Richard A. Smith "awakened about dawn to explosions on the mainland, the word of the Japanese surrender had reached the area and citizens were shooting off fireworks in joyous celebration. Then, and only then, did I think about going home, and it was a great feeling."

Captain Macondray had offered the Nashville to General MacArthur for the surrender ceremonies in Tokyo Bay since the General had so frequently used the ship as his flagship and genuinely liked the ship and crew alike. Word has always been that MacArthur wanted to take Captain Macondray up on the offer but was overruled in favor of the much larger and newer Missouri. We may never know the real reasons for the decision. But for a brief time Nashville did expect to be the ship for the surrender ceremony in Tokyo Bay. Richard A. Smith explains, "The ship was cleaned from bow to stern, repainted powder blue, etc. Due to time constraints he (MacArthur) had to fly to Tokyo and we had a nice, clean, powder blue ship, to the amusement of the rest of the Navy."

Before Nashville got her next orders the crew had their first peacetime liberty since Bermuda in early December 1941. Some men, like Billy Rae Liverly, showed their relief and thankfulness of war's end by attending church and praying, while others took a more straightforward route to expressions of relief. James D. Baccus enjoyed an eventful liberty in Manila. "My buddies and I did some real serious drinking. I swung at something, missed, and hit a steel lamp post, injuring my hand. I was then dared to jump into this canal or river running through Manila. I jumped in but because of my bad hand, had to be rescued. We went back to the ship in a LST that had been hauling cattle, the bottom had water and cow shit all over it. We got into a fight; I wound up having my uniform torn off. When I went aboard I saluted the Officer of the Day with nothing on but my shoes, with my billfold in my left hand."

Rufus B. Thompson Lt. Colonel USMC left the ship on that VJ Day. "The skipper, Captain Macondray said to me that the ship was going to China and I could stay on and he would see that I got air transportation to the States after seeing China. I chose to go to Manila for transportation. I had to stay there in the Manila Hotel, as damaged as it was, and later board one of the Navy hotel ships for three weeks before getting transportation. I caught an Army transport and it took us four weeks to get to the Sates because we were escorting several LSTs, so much for my turning down the offer to go to China."

Nashville was under way again by September 3, headed for Okinawa to become flagship under Rear Admiral C. Turner Joy for Task Force 73. On September 7 she set sail for the recently liberated Chinese city of Shanghai. It was the first time since December 6, 1941 she sailed with full running lights on, lit up like an ocean liner. Nashville arrived off Chusan at the mouth of the Yangtze River on September 9 where she launched scout planes to reconnoiter the area ahead for signs of any threats to the ship. There were none noted so on September 15 Task Force 73, led by Nashville were the first American ships to drop anchor in the Yangtze River since the war started. Elvin Crockett RDM3c remembers sailing up the Yangtze. "Being a radar operator, the first several days were scary since the planes we would pick up, we didn't know if they would attack, otherwise it was an enjoyable time after the Marines disarmed the Japs in the area." But no sooner had they anchored than the entire task force promptly returned to sea in order to avoid a typhoon. Typhoons are not good things for sailors. Richard A. Smith FC3c said "riding out the typhoon" was the worst duty he ever had his entire time in the Navy. "The typhoon had created the heaviest seas I had seen since coming aboard. We were ordered to general quarters and fed meals similar to Army K-rations. I remember going below to bring back a pot of coffee to the others in the gun director. The mess hall was awash with water from broken steam tables, food trays, silverware, tables, and benches washed from one side to the other as the ship rolled and pitched in the storm, the noise was deafening."

Once the typhoon had passed, Task Force 73 returned to the Yangtze where Nashville and Rocky Mount (AGC-3) led the return of the US Navy to Shanghai. The War Diary noted: "The river was crowded with junks and sampans and there was much shouting, blowing of whistles, and waving of Chinese, US, British, and Russian flags." There was no such display of enthusiasm and relief from the rather large contingent of Japanese Army troops lining the river and watching the American procession of ships. Joseph A. Graves SM2c was impressed with the warm and enthusiastic reception. "I have never witnessed anything like that before or since. There were bands playing, horns and sirens blowing, banners strung up as far as you could see, wall to wall people on both sides of the river. People were hanging out of windows."

That morning after the typhoon the Nashville crew resumed (non-firing) testing of her five-inch and six-inch guns that were somewhat damaged during the storm. Richard A. Smith noticed that "as we trained our guns back and forth and up and down we noticed men on the shore running madly for cover. We soon learned there was a POW camp across the river from Shanghai and the Japanese prisoners thought we were about to open fire on them."

On board Nashville, moored in the middle of the Whangpoo River against a background of the Shanghai skyline, Admiral Joy managed the initial stages of taking the Japanese Army into custody and returning them to Japan as well as assisting in the reestablishment of Chinese authority in the area. Shanghai was a relatively decent liberty port with a minimum of war damage so the crew of the Nashville found reasons, legitimate and not so, for going ashore to see things they had never seen before.

Shortly after arriving in Shanghai, Nashville sent a prize crew, including James Clark of the 6th Division and Marine Corporal Stephen L. Saradin, five miles downriver to take over several Japanese ships, including the Koho Maru. Saradin's ship was a Japanese minelayer and the flagship of the group. They did so without incident and soon thereafter handed it over to the Chinese Navy. Meanwhile, the crew experienced liberty in wide open Shanghai. Seventeen-year-old Richard Marelli, who was part of the Nashville football team that beat the Seabees in a game in Shanghai, had a new experience while on liberty. "I was introduced to vodka at the Russian Club in Shanghai, wow!" John W. Bosier met an interesting white Russian woman and went out with her during his liberty.

Sometimes stranger things occurred. Maury Jack Wood SC1c remembers, "One of my fellow shipmates got drunk on liberty and bought a baby for $1.00 and then brought it aboard ship. The officer made him take it back." Shanghai was a wild town touched by the war more in moral and conceptual ways than physical destruction. Small boys approached military personnel trying to get them to come to their homes for sex with their no-doubt underage sisters. Stephen Saradin had a lot of liberty time, enough so as to befriend several families that had a brother in Los Angeles and a sister in San Diego. Later Saradin would kindly deliver letters to them from their Shanghai families.

Gerald T. Jones AMM3c liked the Shanghai liberty. "It was great. No flying to worry about, airplanes were secured, and shore liberty every other day, T-bone steak dinners on shore. I gained about fifteen pounds before we headed back to the States."

Joseph D. Marion S2c was simply amazed to be there. "We could exchange American dollars for large amounts of Chinese Yen. We drank vodka from Coke bottles. I bought souvenirs which I still have, some of which may be valuable. We attended ships' dances, one of which was at the Metropole. Ashore, shipmates took care of their shipmates, I always felt safe there. There was an autumn odor about Shanghai. This did not cover the sites and smells of the Whangpoo River and the sampans moving up and down the river hovering about the ship and coming on board to sell "tailor mades.""

Other sailors, like Vernon G. Mortenson S2c got into trouble in unusual ways. Vernon decided he wanted to help a pedal cab driver out so he had the driver get into the cab section while he pedaled the cab himself. The police did not take well to Vernon's democratic kindness and less so to the driver allowing it to happen. Vernon got the driver out of trouble by buying calling cards written in Chinese from the arresting officer's superior and promising to pick them up the next day, which he did while accompanied by Joseph D. Marion.

Bill Baxter went to a British officer's bar with a Canadian but he was not welcomed by the Brits, only the Canadian was. But to his everlasting credit, Bill's Canadian friend told the Brits, "Where the hell do you think Canada is?" and left with Bill to go drink in the enlisted men's bar.

Richard A. Smith was a member of the Nashville basketball team and one day they went ashore to play a Chinese team of bankers, businessmen, lawyers, and the like. "They were in excellent physical condition and beat us soundly. After the game they entertained us at a seven or eight course banquet and unlimited drinks."

The Nashville also fielded a football team. The ship's Marines found old football uniforms from before the war and the Nashville team of Marines and sailors played an Army team at the famous Shanghai Racetrack. Score: Nashville 12, Army 6. The Midshipman of Annapolis would have been proud.

Shortly before Nashville departed Shanghai hundreds of frozen turkeys were delivered via barge to the ship as she was to be out to sea for the Thanksgiving holiday. It must have seemed like an endless bounty to many of the near-starving junk residents on the Shanghai River.

On November 12, 1945 Admiral Joy departed the ship and Nashville was given orders for the final chapter of her glorious war service, the return of American troops to the United States as part of "Operation Magic Carpet." Wasting no time in her new mission, Nashville embarked 450 troops at Shanghai on a cold, overcast morning with snow flurries on November 13, then sailed to Pearl Harbor where she embarked another ninety troops on November 27 and set course for the United States where she landed with her anxious passengers on December 3 at sunny and warm San Pedro, California. The ship's aviation crews and battle-scarred Marines were transferred ashore to make room for more troops as she was to sail again in a mere six days for Eniwetok for a "capacity personnel lift," otherwise known as taking aboard as many troops as possible regardless of comfort level for guests and crew.

On December 22 Nashville picked up 539 troops and set sail for the United States but first stopping at Kwajalein on Christmas Eve just long enough to embark another 246 eager troops and then set course directly for San Francisco.

Off the coast of San Francisco on January 3, 1946, in a stormy sea, a Nashville radioman picked up a distress signal from the troop transport St. Mary's (APA-126). The transport, with 1,800 veteran Army troops being tossed about on board, had lost her engine and was fighting the rough seas at her best speed of five knots. Nashville steamed immediately to the St. Mary's aid and maneuvered into position to shoot her a tow line (no mean feat in the stormy seas) at 0730. By 0903 Nashville had secured St. Mary's with a tow line and commenced towing her at a maximum safe speed of exactly six point two knots. By 1935 hours Nashville was sending visual signals via twenty-four-inch searchlight to US Navy tugs. Joseph D. Marion S2c was in the thick of it, "I found myself using the TBS to talk to someone on the St. Mary's about the tautness of the tow lines. Again, I was amazed at what I was doing and that I knew how to do it. I saw a plane hovering about as we approached the coast. It turned out it was taking pictures, one of which appeared in the *New York Times* with the full story. My mother obtained a glossy which I still have." The distant sailor on the flying bridge of the Nashville in that photograph is most likely Joseph D. Marion. Eventually, St. Mary's and her troops lumbered into San Francisco Bay where Navy tugs nestled her to the safety of a dock on January 6.

As Nashville entered San Francisco Bay herself, so many sailors, soldiers, and Marines went topside to see San Francisco's welcoming skyline the ship listed noticeably to starboard. She anchored 200 yards south of Berth 7 in San Francisco Bay among many other warships including USS Oakland. She took on such provisions as sixty gallons of ice cream, 525 pounds of bread, 450 pounds of radishes, 800 pounds of grapes and 200 gallons of milk. She also had minor repair work done on the tips of #1 screw which were bent about an inch or two.

At Mare Island, where she was provisioned, armed and readied for the Doolittle Raid almost four years prior, she was prepared for her final voyage as a fighting ship of the United States Navy. She was placed on keel blocks in dry-dock #3. At 0510 Nashville slipped out of her flooded dry-dock in Mare Island and then the tugs cast off at 0549, leaving Nashville completely under her own power and control at the beginning of the end of her Navy service. At 0735 on January 21, 1946, she passed under the Golden Gate Bridge as she had on the Doolittle Raid, although this would be the last she would ever see of San Francisco. She made course for Philadelphia and the mothball fleet, traversing the Panama Canal on January 29-30. On February 4 she arrived in Philadelphia and received a pre-inactivation overhaul as final preparation for mothballing. Charles A. Foley FC1c had been on board since January 1942 and was on board at the end as part of a sixty-plus man maintenance crew. Nashville was appropriately moored alongside a sister ship, USS Phoenix. How far they had come after sailing together through many dark days in the Solomons and later throughout the Pacific, as the tide of war turned in America's favor. It was suitable they both came to rest together among scores of others being mothballed in Philadelphia. Most of the crew was of course transferred to other duties and ships, but many of those found an excuse to stop and say good-bye in their own way. Joe Fales was transferred to the USS Ranger in Philadelphia so he stopped by to visit, looking at the Nashville in mothballs and running into an old crew mate, Harland Price, Boatswains Mate in the 2nd Division. Ron Nickerson and a friend were the last two men to leave the ship on decommissioning. "It was like leaving home," said Ron.

By Directive in March 1946 the ship was designated for disposal as surplus according to Navy needs. Those needs had not yet been specified. On June 24, 1946 at 1400 the stroke of a government pen did what the Japanese had tried, claimed, and failed to do for four years, her commissioning pennant was hoisted down and she was decommissioned and out of service to crew, Navy, and country.

But the story does not end with her decommissioning. As part of an American plan to assist South American countries in strengthening their ability to defend themselves against communist aggression, six American light cruisers were designated for sale to the navies of Chile, Brazil, and Argentina. On January 9, 1951 she was sold to Chile and was permanently struck from the Navy list on November 22, 1951. And still, that is not the end of her saga of seafaring duty.

Nashville band practicing in the ship's hanger

Herbert "Herb" (& Jean Taylor), 12/44, Boarded January 43/Left Oct 44

Fred Varni

Nashville Boxing Club

Men ashore, Admiralty Islands

Band on the hanger deck

Billy Ray Lyerly, Chief at age 22

"E" Division, Shanghai 1945

Captain Wentworth, 1940

George L. Bustin, served over 3 ½ years aboard Nashville

EPILOGUE
Taps for a Great Ship

***

"Every time I see an American flag flying I am reminded of all service men and women who have died for their country during wartime. I pray it does not happen again."
-Charles R. Conrad

***

During WWII a total of seventy-four American cruisers engaged in battle and yet today not a single cruiser survives either in a mothball fleet or as a museum. Unlike veterans of battleships, aircraft carriers, and even a few Liberty ships, Nashville and other cruiser veterans can not reminisce aboard their old ships. Rather, their ship lives only in hearts and minds.

Few ships in American naval history reap the rewards and respect of service to their crew and country. Some notably historic ships such as the Constitution, Arizona, Missouri, and Hornet are gratefully preserved as museums and memorials for the public. Most ships are scrapped, especially after a war as the country is eager to move on to a new era and crew exchange uniforms for "civvies." Others are sold to countries seeking dated but functional warships for their own navies. Such was the inglorious fate of the USS Nashville. After she completed her immediate postwar duty as a troop transport bringing America's fighting men back home, she proceeded to Philadelphia Navy Yard for mothballing. She remained in this comatose state until 1952 when she was prepared for a one way trip to Chile. She was stripped of her suddenly outdated catapults and planes, replaced by a functional, modern helicopter pad that would never launch aircraft against a determined enemy. In 1957, twenty years after she was launched, Nashville returned to the United States for modernization, receiving the latest radar and sonar as well as new upgraded masts. Serving in the Chilean navy first as the O'Brian and later renamed the Capitan Pratt after Chile's most revered naval hero, Nashville participated in several salvage operations and UNITAS ("unity") operations, a multinational navy operation of the countries of the Americas. She also did what she had done so many times before, serve as a flagship.

At 0538 Hours on April 1, 1971, while steaming forty miles due west of Puerto Aldez, she was accidentally rammed amidships by the destroyer Cochrane. The impact opened a sixteen-foot wide, four-foot high gash in her side between the smokestacks, right at the second boiler room below the waterline. After fifteen minutes of the damage control team fighting the inflow of seawater which rose to their necks, the boiler room was abandoned as well as the adjoining room. Emergency power systems kicked into action as the damage control crews reinforced the bulkheads, reminiscent of the Biak near miss action of 1942. Once again the ship was saved by damage control and she limped into Talcahuan for dry-dock repairs. It was almost a year by the time the ship rejoined the Chilean Fleet.

On her fiftieth birthday, the ship fired several full-battery broadsides, hitting every single target. In 1987, once again she faced decommissioning, having served a full forty-two years past her expected service lifetime. While the myth is that the Nashville sank in a storm while being towed to Taiwan for scrap, this author could discern no evidence of that whatsoever. However, her sister ship the Brooklyn (O'Higgins in the Chilean Navy) did in fact sink in a storm while under tow and this may be the source of the misinformation. After decommissioning, the Nashville (Capitan Prat) was renamed the Chacabuco and used as an accommodation hulk. But those in the Chilean Navy still referred to her as El Prat Viejo (the Old Prat). Finally, the end came for Nashville on April 29, 1983 when she was sold to Canadian businessman Noel Williams Kennedy and then towed to Kaoshiung, Taiwan, that country's largest industrial center and second largest city. Nashville finally ended her useful life in the Pacific where she had made such a tremendous contribution to freedom and liberty during WWII. May she ever rest in peace.

LIST OF COMMANDING OFFICERS

***

Captain William W. Wilson USN 6 June 38-1 Jan. 40
Captain Ralph S. Wentworth USN 1 Jan. 40-30 April 41
Captain Francis S. Craven USN 1 May 41-30 Sept. 42
Captain Herman A. Spanagel USN 30 Sept. 42-25 Apr 44
Captain Charles E. Coney USN 25 Apr 44-30 Jan. 45
Commander John T. Corwin USN 30 Jan. 45-21 Mar 45
Captain Atherton Macondray, Jr. USN 21 March 45-34 Jan. 46

USS NASHVILLE (CL-43) FACT SHEET

***

Light Cruiser Class: Brooklyn

Displacement 9,475 Tons, Dimensions, 608' 4" x 61' 8" x 24'

Armament 15 x 6"/47, 8 x 5"/25, 8 x 0.5" 4 Aircraft

Armor, 5" Belt, 6 ½" Turrets, 2" Deck, 5" Conning Tower

Machinery, 100,000 SHP; Geared Turbines, 4 screws

Speed, 32.5 Knots, Crew 868

Keel laid on 24 January 1935 by the New York Shipbuilding Corp., Camden, NJ

Launched 02 October 1937

Commissioned 06 June1938

Decommissioned 24 June1946 Stricken 9 January 1961

Transferred to the Chilean Navy 9 January 1951 and renamed Capitan Prat, then renamed Chacabuco

Decommissioned 10 May 1982

Ultimate Fate: Sold for scrap 29 April 1983 to Canadian Noel Williams Kennedy and towed to Kaohshiung,Taiwan

POSTSCRIPT
The USS Nashville Reunion Association

***

"We endured the bloody kamikaze attack during WWII, now our enemy is time."
-William R. Banks Jr.

***

Interest in forming some sort of group or reunion association occurred not too many years after the war. It is only natural for men, who formed a bond under war conditions, bound by total interdependence on their very survival, who jointly shared the most mundane daily routines and most horrific events of death, all as vibrant young men, would want to maintain a structure that helped them keep those very special bonds alive.

For decades "Bulldog" and Audrey Remler in Overland Park, Kansas were the guardians and driving force behind Nashville memories and the Reunion Association. "Bulldog" is a man with a gentle and congenial personality unbefitting his nickname, at least in civilian life. Being centrally located in the heartland of the country, their home became a waypoint for many Nashville travelers. More than a few would stop and stay a day or a week or more each spring and fall as they traveled on annual vacations. At times, more than ten to twelve people would be present, making for some great parties. The Remler basement became a Nashville library as more and more of the crew and their families sent newspaper clippings, letters, stories, photographs, and mementos. On hand is the Homeward Bound pennant from the ship, a letter from Mrs. Douglas MacArthur, ship's rosters, and the like. The official USS Nashville collection, housed in a wing of the WWII Museum in the namesake city of Nashville, Tennessee, is only marginally more impressive in scope, but perhaps not in memories.

As of this writing, the Remlers, due to the inevitable health problems facing us all as we get older, have passed the baton to Don and Goldie Hill of New Mexico, who have hosted the reunions for several years now. Don served aboard Nashville as a handsome young Marine and his photo was used as a recruiting poster in 1943.

To this day, when the crew speaks of the Nashville and their shipmates, both present and gone, they do so with a gleam in the eye and a strong place in the heart. Unlike an infantry regiment that moves from one foxhole to another, village to village, and even country to country during the war, the men on a ship, while they are on that ship, are always in the same town, always at home no matter how far from port they may be. The ship is a tightly confined and highly structured home town segmented into smaller divisions and groups driven by responsibilities and duties and hence, location. They all are totally interdependent on the most basic things, from eating to sleeping to daily routines and life itself. They literally live, fight, and die in their home. Speak with any sailor or Marine that spent any long period aboard a ship and see how they speak of "she" as if it were a living thing and of course, in all but biological terms, "she" is.

As the crew aged and more and more became sick, unable to travel, and passed away, there was talk that maybe the end of reunions was getting near, that maybe there would not be enough members physically able to attend, that the association had served its purpose and maybe the next reunion, in Branson, Missouri in 2004 would be the last. Any such thoughts were mitigated upon the members receiving the following letter from one of their most respected and loved crewmates, Captain Leonard "Len" Meyer.

"Dear Shipmates and friends. I am deeply disappointed that I am unable to attend this great USS Nashville (CL43) reunion in Branson. I have always looked forward to these interesting and wonderful gatherings. However, due to 'Macular Degeneration' in both eyes, I am not able to read or write without the aid of a large magnifying glass, or to travel without someone to depend upon to see that I get to where I should be.

I am sure all who attend the reunion will be well repaid with renewed friendships and the many excellent shows in Branson. Most of all it is the fellowship that takes place at the USS Nashville (CL43) reunions that unite us all into one big wonderful family. In my 22+ years of navy life I have never experienced a happier or more closely knit family-like crew than that of the USS Nashville (CL43).

If it wasn't for shipmates and friends like you, I think I would lose my faith in Man, you always have had a cheery word for me and always understand. Your actions speak louder than your words ever do: I know I am blessed just for knowing you. So today I want to tell you in case you might not know, how very much your friendship means the older I grow (I am approaching 93)".

Captain Meyer did not make that 2004 Branson, Missouri reunion, but with the assistance of his son and to the great satisfaction of the crew, he proudly attended the 2005 reunion in Cincinnati, Ohio and the 2006 reunion in Washington, DC.

The Reunion Newsletter that is published by Don and Goldie Hill three to four times each year has the homey feeling of a small-town newspaper. It includes general announcements, the financial statement for the organization, notes, cards, letters, and emails from members on such things as additions to the family and travel plans, changes of address, illnesses, and a section titled "Taps" for those that passed on. It is a lifeline for many members, especially those unable to attend reunions.

Marine John Mane reminisces during the 2003 reunion in Nashville, TN

Ronald Nickerson and his grandson at WWII Memorial during
reunion of September 2006

Don and Goldie Hill with author, Washington D.C. Reunion
September 2006

BIBLIOGRAPHY

***

Adcock, Al. *US Light Cruisers in Action*. Carrollton. Squadron/Signal Publications, 1999.

Agawa, Hiroyuki. *The Reluctant Admiral*. Trans. John Bester. Tokyo: Kodansha, 2000.

Allen, Thomas B. and Norman Polmar. *Code-Name Downfall: The Secret Plan to Invade Japan and Why Truman Dropped the Bomb*. New York: Simon, 1995.

Alexander, Joseph H. *What Was Nimitz Thinking?*
United States Naval Institute. *Proceedings*; Annapolis; Nov 1998.

Beigel, Harvey M. Battleship Country: *The Battle Fleet at San Pedro—Long Beach, California*, 1919-1940. Missoula: Pictorial, 1983.

Bernstein, Marc D. Hurricane at Biak: *MacArthur against the Japanese*, May-August 1944. Sunnyvale: Bernstein, 2000.

Bernstein, Marc D. *Tin Cans Raid* Balikpapan.
United States Naval Institute. *Proceedings*; Annapolis; April 2003.

Binns, Stewart and Adrian Wood. *America at War in Color: Unique Images of the American Experience in World War II*. London: Carlton, 2001.

Bix, Herbert P. *Hirohito and the Making of Modern Japan*. New York: Harper, 2000.

Blair, Clay Jr. *MacArthur*. New York: Nelson, 1977.

Bonner, Kit and Carolyn Bonner. *Warship Boneyards*. Osceola: MBI, 2001.

Bradley, James and Ron Powers. *Flags of Our Fathers*. New York: Bantam, 2000.

Bradley, James. *Flyboys: A True Story of Courage*. New York: Back Bay, 2004.

Center of Military History, United States Army. *The War against Japan*. Washington: Brassey's, 1998.

Cohen, Stan. Destination: Tokyo: *A Pictorial History of Doolittle's Tokyo Raid April 18, 1942*. Missoula: Pictorial, 1998.

Cutler, Thomas J. *Greatest of All Sea Battles*.

United States Naval Institute. *Proceedings*; Annapolis; Sep/Oct 1994.

Ewing, Steve. *American Cruisers of World War II: A Pictorial Encyclopedia*. Missoula: Pictorial, 2000.

Garfield, Brian. *The Thousand-Mile War: World War II in Alaska and the Aleutians*. Fairbanks: Alaska UP, 1995.

Cook, Haruko Taya and Theodore F. Cook. *Japan At War: An Oral History*. New York: New, 1992.

Cutler, Thomas J. *The Battle of Leyte Gulf: 23-26 October, 1944*. Annapolis: Naval, 2001.

Davis, James Martin and Bert Webber. *Top Secret: The Details of the Planned World War II Invasion of Japan and How the Japanese Would Have Met It*: Documentary. Medford: Webb, 1998.

Dull, Paul S. *A Battle History of the Imperial Japanese Navy (1941-1945)*. Annapolis: Naval, 1978.

Dunnigan, James F. and Albert A. Nofi. *Victory at Sea: World War II in the Pacific*. New York: Morrow, 1995.

Fensch, Thomas, ed. *Top Secret World War II: U.S. Military Plans for the Invasion of Japan*. The Woodlands: New, 2001.

Frank, Richard B. Downfall: *The End of the Imperial Japanese Empire*. New York: Penguin, 2001.

Generous, William Thomas Jr. *Sweet Pea at War: A History of USS Portland*. Lexington: Kentucky UP, 2003.

Goldstein, Donald M. and Katherine V. Dillon, ed. *The Pearl Harbor Papers: Inside the Japanese Plans*. Washington: Brassey's, 2000.

Goldstein, Donald M., Katherine V. Dillon, and J. Michael Wenger. *The Way It Was:_Pearl Harbor—The Original Photographs*. Washington: Brassey's, 1995.

Greene, Bob. Duty: *A Father, His Son, and the Man Who Won the War*. New York: Morrow, 2000.

Halsey, William F. *USS Enterprise Action Report* (Serial 0019)-18 April 1942.

United States Naval Archives

Hammond, James W. Jr. The Treaty Navy: *The Story of the US Naval Service between the World Wars*. Victoria: Trafford, 2001.

Hanson, Victor Davis. Carnage and Culture: *Landmark Battles in the Rise of Western Power.* New York: Doubleday, 2001.

Hanson, Victor Davis. *The Soul of Battle: From Ancient Times to the Present Day, How Three Great Liberators Vanquished Tyranny.* New York: Free, 1999.

Haris, Richard. *Hell in the Pacific-from Vivisection to Cannibalism.* San Francisco Chronicle, March 17, 2002.

Hornfischer, James D. *The Last Stand of the Tin Can Sailors: The Extraordinary World War II Story of the U.S. Navy's Finest Hour.* New York: Bantam, 2004.

Howser, W.D. *While MacArthur Slept*
Naval History, Annapolis: Sept/Oct 1997.

Inoguchi, Captain Rikihei, Commander Tadashi Nakajima, Roger Pineau. *The Divine Wind: Japan's Kamikaze Force in World War II.* Annapolis: Naval, 1994.

Lotchin, Roger W. *The Bad City in the Good War: San Francisco, Los Angeles, Oakland, and San Diego.* Bloomington: Indiana UP, 2003.

Lunstrom, John. *The War with Japan: The Period of Balance,* May 1942-October 1943.

United States Naval Institute. *Proceedings,* Annapolis Jun 2002.

MacArthur, Douglas. *Reminiscences: General of the Army.* Annapolis: Naval, 2001..

Maga, Tim. *America Attacks Japan: The Invasion That Never Was.* Lexington: Kentucky UP, 2002.

Manchester, William. *Goodbye, Darkness: A Memoir of the Pacific War.* Boston: Little, 1980.

Morison, Samuel Eliot. *History of United States Naval Operations in World War II.* 14 vols. Edison: Castle, 2001.

Morison, Samuel Eliot. *History of United States Naval Operations in World War II. Supplement and General Index.* Edison: Castle, 2001.

Muray, George D. *USS Enterprise Action Report (Serial 088)*-18 April 1942.

Nelson, Craig. *The First Heroes: The Extraordinary Story of the Doolittle Raid—America's First World War II Victory.* New York: Penguin, 2003.

Newcombe, Dick. *U.S Destroyers of the World Wars: History of the "Tin Cans."* Paducah: Turner, 1994.

Nimitz, Chester. Halsey-Doolittle Raid: *Bombing of Tokyo*, April 24-29 1942.

O'Donnell, Patrick K. Beyond Valor: *World War II's Ranger and Airborne Veterans Reveal the Heart of Combat*. New York: Free, 2001.
O'Donnell, Patrick K. *Into the Rising Sun: In Their Own Words, World War II's Pacific Veterans Reveal the Heart of Combat*. New York: Free, 2002.
Osborne, Richard E. *World War II Sites in the United States: A Tour Guide and Directory*. Indianapolis: Riebel-Roque, 1996.
Oxford, Edward. Jimmy Doolittle: "Against All Odds"
American History Magazine, August 1997.

Prados, John. *Combined Fleet: The Secret History of American Intelligence and the Japanese Navy in World War II*. New York: Random, 1995.
Prange, Gordon W. *At Dawn We Slept: The Untold Story of Pearl Harbor*. New York: McGraw, 1981.
Riley, John Powel Jr. *Radar Capabilities and Limitations*, 1944.
US Navy Publications, United States Naval Institute, July/August 1998.
Rose, Lisle A. *The Ship That Held the Line: The USS Hornet and the First Year of the Pacific War*. Annapolis: Naval, 2002.
Rottman, Gordon L. *Japanese Pacific Island Defenses 1941-45*. Oxford: Osprey, 2003.
Sakai, Saburo. *Samurai!*
iBooks, Inc 1957.

Sides, Hampton. *Ghost Soldiers: The Forgotten Epic Story of World War II's Most Dramatic Mission*. New York: Doubleday, 2001.
Spaulding, G. H. The Doolittle Raid: "How America Responded to the Sneak Attack on Pearl Harbor," *Centennial Aviation and Business Journal*, Jan 2001.
Spector, Ronald H. *At War at Sea: Sailors And Naval Combat in the Twentieth Century*. Viking Penguin, 2001.
Stanton, Doug. *In Harm's Way: The Sinking of the USS Indianapolis and the Extraordinary Story of its Survivors*. New York: Henry, 2001.
Taaffe, Stephen R. *MacArthur's Jungle War: The 1944 New Guinea Campaign*. Lawrence: Kansas UP, 1998.

Tanaka, Yuki. Hidden Horrors: *Japanese War Crimes In World War II*. Boulder: Westview, 1998.

The First Radio Broadcasts from Ships
http://www.offshore-radio.de/fleet/first5.htm

Time, Inc. V-J Day: *America's World War II Triumph in the Pacific*. New York: Time, 2005.

Toppan, Andrew. US Cruisers List: Light/Heavy/Antiaircraft Cruisers, Part 1
http://www.hazegray.org, January 2000.

Whitley, M.J. *Cruisers of World War Two: An International Encyclopedia*. Annapolis: Naval, 2000.

William H. Wise & Co., Inc. Battle Stations: Your Navy in Action. New York: Wise, 1946.

Worth, Richard. *Fleets of World War II*. Cambridge, Da Capo, 2001.

Ugaki, Matome. *Fading Victory: The Diary of Admiral Matome Ugaki, 1941-1945*. Ed. Donald M. Goldstein and Katherine V. Dillon, Trans. Masatake Chihaya. Pittsburgh: Pittsburgh UP, 1991.

van der Vant, Dan. *Attack at Pearl Harbor, 1941, Eye Witness-History through the Eyes of Those Who Lived It*. http://www.ibiscom.com 1997.

van der Vant, Dan. *The Pacific Campaign: The U.S.-Japanese Naval War 1941-1945*. New York: Touchstone, 1992

***

AUTHORS NOT CITED

Action Report
Task Group 2.7
Serial 477, 21 August 1941
Neutrality Patrol Operations, 6-19 August 1941, National Archives and Records Administration, Modern Military Records (NWCTM), Textual Archives Services Division.

Action Report

Task Group 2.7
Serial C-151, 10 September 1941, *Neutrality Patrol Operations, 28 August-9 September 1941*, National Archives and Records Administration, Modern Military Records (NWCTM), Textual Archives Services Division.

Action Report

USS Nashville CL43
Serial None, 24 September 1941
Operational Report, National Archives and Records Administration, Modern Military Records (NWCTM), Textual Archives Services Division.

Action Report

Serial 01450, 19 May 1942
Grounding Of USS Nashville At Midway, National Archives and Records Administration, Modern Military Records (NWCTM), Textual Archives Services Division.

Action Report

USS Nashville CL43
Serial 0011, 15 July 1944

War Damage Report

National Archives and Records Administration

Modern Military Records (NWCTM)
Textual Archives Services Division

Action Report

USS Nashville CL43
Serial 0128, 20 October 1944
National Archives and Records Administration, Modern Military Records
(NWCTM), Textual Archives Services Division

Action Report

USS Nashville CL43
Serial 0125, 1 November 1944

Report of Anti-aircraft Action Covering Action While in Leyte Gulf In Task Unit 77.1.2

National Archives and Records Administration, Modern Military Records
(NWCTM), Textual Archives Services Division

Action Report

USS Nashville CL43
Serial 0132, 15 November 1944
Report of Anti-aircraft Action From 1 November 1944 to 2 November 1944,
National, Archives and Records Administration, Modern Military
Records (NWCTM), Textual Archives Services Division.

Action Report

USS Nashville CL43
Serial 06, 8 January 1945
Report of Anti-aircraft Action 13 December 1944. Forwards AA
Form Report Covering Action on 13 December 1944 While in Sulu
Sea, National Archives and Records Administration, Modern Military
Records (NWCTM), Textual Archives Services Division

Action Report

USS Nashville CL43

29 July 1945
National Archives and Records Administration, Modern Military Records
(NWCTM), Textual Archives Services Division

Anonymous. The Halsey-Doolittle Raid

Naval History Annapolis May/Jun 1995

Anonymous. Plank Owners

Department of the Navy-Naval Historical Center, Washington DC, January 1996

Consulate General of Chile, San Francisco, California, USA

Consulate General of Japan, San Francisco, California, USA

Crossing the Line, Plank Owner and Other Unofficial Certificates Acquired by Naval Personnel
Department of the Navy-Naval Historical Center, Washington DC, April 2001

Deck Logs

USS Nashville CL43
22 September 22 1938
Shipment of Gold Bullion for Bank of England, National Archives and Records Administration, Modern Military Records (NWCTM), Textual Archives Services Division

Deck Logs

USS Nashville CL43
January 3-9, 1946
National Archives and Records Administration, Modern Military Records (NWCTM), Textual Archives Services Division

Deck Logs

USS Nashville CL43

June 24, 1946
National Archives and Records Administration, Modern Military Records (NWCTM), Textual Archives Services Division

Dictionary of American Naval Fighting Ships. 9 vols.

Washington: Naval Historical Center, 1959-1991

List of Official US Navy Certificates

Department of the Navy-Naval Historical Center, Washington DC, March 2002

Navy Department Communiques December 1941-December 1943

United States Naval Archives

Navy Department Communiques December 1943-February 1945

United States Naval Archives

Ships Present at Pearl Harbor, 0800 7 December 1941

Department of the Navy-Naval Historical Center

Washington DC, National Archives and Records Administration, Modern Military Records (NWCTM), Textual Archives Services Division

United States Strategic Bombing Survey Summary Report (Pacific War)

United States Government Printing Office, Washington DC, 1 July 1946

War Damage Report
USS Nashville CL43
Serial 0015, 7 July 1944
Report of War Damage Sustained As A Result of Anti-aircraft Action Off Biak, Schouten Islands, 4 June 1944, National Archives and Records Administration, Modern Military Records (NWCTM), Textual Archives Services Division

War Diary

USS Nashville CL43
December 7-31 1941
National Archives and Records Administration, Modern Military Records (NWCTM), Textual Archives Services Division

War Diaries

USS Nashville CL43
May 2-4 1942

Memorandum: Raid on Japanese Fishing Fleet Operating East of Kamchatka, National Archives and Records Administration, Modern Military Records (NWCTM), Textual Archives Services Division

War Diaries

USS Nashville CL43
May 7- June 1, 1942
National Archives and Records Administration, Modern Military Records (NWCTM), Textual Archives Services Division

War Diary For January (5-11) 1945

USS Nashville CL43

National Archives and Records Administration, Modern Military Records (NWCTM), Textual Archives Services Division

War Diary

USS Nashville CL43

July 9, 1945
National Archives and Records Administration, Modern Military Records (NWCTM), Textual Archives Services Division

World War II-Asiatic-Pacific Theater 1941-1946

Department of the Navy, Naval Historical Center, Washington DC December 2000